Also by Thalassa Cruso

Making Things Grow:
   A Practical Guide to Indoor Gardening

Making Things Grow Outdoors

To Everything There Is a Season:
   The Gardening Year

Making
Vegetables
Grow

Wood engravings by JAMES GRASHOW

Making Vegetables Grow

Thalassa Cruso

Alfred · A · Knopf · New York

To
New Home-Vegetable Growers
    Everywhere

Contents

Acknowledgments

No book of this sort is ever put together without the assistance of many people who made a far greater contribution to it than is properly served by a brief acknowledgment such as this. Unfortunately, all those who deserve it cannot have their names on the title page. This short listing in no way does justice to the help I've received. First, of course, my deepest thanks are due to Mr. James Grashow, the illustrator who created the enchanting wood engravings. They bring a strength and clarity which is invaluable to the text. I am also enormously indebted to my many gardening friends whom I have pestered with questions during the past months: in particular to those magnificent vegetable growers Mr. Albert Bigelow, Mr. Jerome Eaton, Mrs. Calvin Hosmer, and Major Henry Forester. It is hard to find the proper words with which to thank my editor, Jane Garrett, herself an avid vegetable grower. She prodded me into undertaking this book, did her usual brilliant editorial job, and added a new dimension to the enormous debt I owe her by producing invaluable firsthand information concerning short-season crops in Vermont. My agent, Ellen Neuwald, as ever provided the goad, the spur, and the balm when my spirit needed it. I am grateful to my secretary, Joan Dickey,

who performed heroic service under pressure that was not of her making, to Camilla Filancia, who designed the book, to Mildred Owen, who copyedited it and whose horticultural knowledge was a tremendous bonus, and to Anne Eberle, who undertook the always exasperating and frustrating job of making the index.

The many hidden hands at Alfred A. Knopf, Inc., who speeded up the production of the book should also receive warm thanks. If this book encourages new gardeners to try their hand with vegetables it will have served its purpose and made all this unsung effort, and mine, thoroughly worthwhile.

Thalassa Cruso

Boston, 1975

Making Vegetables Grow

Introduction

 When I was small my family lived in London. We had a house with a back-yard in which my parents created a pleasant little garden. It had a patch of grass, a flower bed along a sunny wall with roses scrambling up posts, and there were ferns and shrubs along the shady side. The garden was something of a showpiece, and the family was justifiably proud of it. But to my youthful eyes it had a very great weakness compared with my grandparents' garden: it had no vegetables; nothing fresh or juicy came from it to go to the kitchen. Looking back, I think this was not just the greedy reaction of a small child; it was something rather more fundamental. I worked alongside my father in that little London garden, I was interested in the flowers and his success with them, but at my grandfather's I spent a lot of time in the kitchen garden, partly, of course, to pillage the fruit, but also watching with delight as fat cabbage, long carrots, and thick asparagus spikes were harvested for the table. And in consequence, our garden in town seemed to be only half a garden, since it was devoted only to flowers. When later my family moved to the country and included a vegetable garden in their horticultural activities, I lost that sense of incompleteness—the family garden had all I needed in it.

Something of that feeling still lingers with me now. I love potted plants, flower beds, shrubs, and trees, and I am reasona-

bly devoted to well-kept lawns, but when I'm invited to look over other people's yards my deepest interest lies in their vegetable plots. The presence, or absence, of space devoted to growing vegetables, not to mention the appearance of those same vegetables, tells me more about the gardener than any other part of the yard.

Growing vegetables is not the easiest of gardening activities. I have been at it in the United States for over thirty years, and I still have an enormous amount to learn. With ornamental gardening, a few flowers in bloom can go a long way, and a failure is not all that important. With vegetable gardening, virtually the entire crop must succeed if the gardener's efforts are not to have been in vain. What's more, in a small plot several successive crops must come to a lavish harvest, almost all of them grown from seed, something very few people ever attempt these days with their flowers. With vegetables you also need more specific knowledge than with flowers. You have to take better care of the soil, discover how to keep its fertility high, and learn how to live with the spoilers, the pests and predators that may descend upon you. With vegetables you cannot be a casual gardener; you must be on hand much of the time, not only to work the land and to keep the crops coming, but also to harvest them before they spoil.

All this is much more demanding than setting out a few annual plants bought from the garden center, but to me it is also enormously more rewarding. The most obvious reason is, of course, the taste of home-grown vegetables. There's absolutely no comparison between them and any that are store-bought, and that is why I would like to encourage people who feel that they have no space for vegetables to *make* space, if only by growing certain amenable crops, like tomatoes and cucumbers and many herbs in containers in any sunny spot anywhere. If you have a really large area, you may also save some money by vegetable gardening, and not only during the growing season, but also in the winter, by processing and storing surplus crops. But even in inflation-ridden times this will not automatically be the case; you will have to work at keeping your costs down even with a garden. It takes a lot of effort and work and quite a large garden to feed a family of four

from your own vegetable plot even during the summer growing season. So, if you calculate your time into the total cost, the saving of money really should not be a primary consideration for taking up vegetable growing, or you may be disappointed. To me the importance of a vegetable garden is the fact that all the family can be a part of it, since they enjoy the harvest that the gardener has enjoyed raising. There are very few other gardening activities in which all the family are involved, even in this rather left-handed manner.

I made my first American vegetable garden in 1942 in climatic Zone 5 (average annual minimum temperature of -10 to -5 degrees). Five years later, with a certain amount of accumulated experience, I started a vegetable garden in Zone 6 (average annual minimum temperature of -5 to 5 degrees) where it still flourishes. Over the years the plot has expanded, contracted, and recently reexpanded according to the number of people I am feeding. I've changed my style of vegetable growing radically over the years, and each season I try out some new varieties of vegetables or new methods. Vegetable gardening is a continuing experiment, which is what makes it both a pleasure and a challenge. It is also a very forgiving experience. Vegetables, with a few exceptions, are all annuals, so each year you can start afresh with a clean slate, no matter how horrendous your mistakes the previous season. With vegetables there is always another chance to do better the next time.

Vegetable growing can test your stamina and your perseverance, and I do not think it fair to minimize this with would-be vegetable gardeners. It can, and will, cut into your free time much more than any other gardening activity, for vegetable growing is not a job you can begin and then neglect and still have any success.

This book deals with the basic processes that are needed to raise vegetables. The time when you sow certain seeds and the varieties used will, of course, differ in different climates and in different areas of the country, but the principles are the same everywhere. And it's in mastering these principles, and bringing the end results of a new skill to your table, that you will discover the huge satisfaction of growing vegetables.

Site and Size

Once you have decided to grow vegetables, the first job is to find a suitable place in the yard. Vegetables, unfortunately, are much fussier in their needs than a bed of petunias and marigolds, and in order to avoid disappointments, it is wise to realize this before you begin. Vegetables will bend a little to accommodate themselves to the growing conditions you have to offer, but to a much more limited degree than flowers. And there are some requirements that simply must be met if the time and effort involved are to be worthwhile.

There are, for example, blossoming shrubs and flowers that prefer to grow in light shade, but there are no such vegetables. This means that any vegetable plot needs a large amount of sunlight. It is sometimes said that any area that will grow weeds will also grow vegetables. Perhaps so—initially. But vegetables take a great deal of goodness out of the ground, for if they are to make any sort of dent in the family grocery bill and not just serve as a gourmet delight they must grow to a good size or bear a large harvest. This means that any area that is to grow a hearty crop of vegetables must start off each season with a deep, rich, well-balanced soil, rather better than we bother about for most flowers. And the **soil fertility** must be kept high if you intend to grow more than one crop and garden more than one season. But if your soil is not sufficiently good

it can be made so; and for that reason soil fertility and quality are not such vital considerations as sunlight when it comes to site selection.

To produce a worthwhile harvest, vegetables also need adequate **moisture** regularly available. A plant raised by steady growth, without thirsty periods when it lacks water, will be more tasty than those which suffer from periodic droughts. This is especially true of root crops such as beets and carrots. Nature is an unreliable ally in this matter and cannot be counted on always to supply the necessary moisture in the right amounts and times. Any place where vegetables are to be raised must have a reliable water supply nearby. If your most appropriate garden site is not close to an existing hose connection, it is important to bring the water to it in one way or another. This need not involve dragging lengths of hose across the yard, for inexpensive plastic pipe with a hose fitting on the end can be set just below ground level and survive even bitter winter cold.

So what about the site? With so many requirements where should it be placed? The first essential is that the plot get as much **sun** as possible. Vegetables thrive everywhere in full sun all day, and this is particularly true of areas where the growing season is short. The least they can tolerate is six hours of full sun and bright light—not shade—for the remaining daylight hours. If there is a choice between a place that gets early morning sun against one that gets afternoon sun, choose the position with morning sun. Plants make better use of morning sunlight for the process of photosynthesis (the conversion into plant food, through an energy process, of the minerals they have drawn in with the moisture through their roots) than they do in the blazing heat of afternoon sun. If you simply do not possess a spot that has full sun all day, you must make up your mind that some crops will not prosper as well as they do in a neighbor's sun-drenched plot.

But in spite of this emphasis on the importance of a lot of sun, do not be put off trying to grow any vegetables because your garden is not as brilliantly sunlit as a baseball field. Don't forget that British gardeners raise wonderful crops of certain

vegetables with far less hot sunshine than even a shaded lot over here can get. The trick to growing vegetables in a less than perfect place where sunlight is concerned is to choose very carefully what you try to grow. Leaf crops such as lettuce, chard, spinach, and kale, for example, require less sunlight than vegetables which must develop edible roots or fruits. With discrimination you will still be able to eat well from your own plot. But if you are going to use a place with less than full sunlight, it pays to walk around your yard, possibly even with a compass in hand, and see whether there is not some other small area, a strip of unused land, space beside a garage wall or a boundary fence that faces due south and where it would be possible to dig up and enrich the soil to make a deep bed for the heat- and sun-demanding plants. Tomatoes and cucumbers will both do excellently in such a place and can be trained up a wire trellis fixed against a wall. Melons can be raised in homemade cold frames, or in the small metal cold frames that are available from garden stores, filled with plenty of rich soil and set in just such a warm place with the open bottom of the box standing on dug-up ground.

Vegetables Requiring the Least Sun

Chard	Mint
Chicory	Parsley
Collards	Peas
Kale	Scarlet Runner Beans
Lettuce	Spinach

If the only place in your yard that gets the right exposure is the front lawn, I would put the vegetable plot there. Front lawns are very little used. Most family activities go on behind the house in a less public setting, and to turn an otherwise

useless piece of ground into a good growing area makes perfect sense. I put my first U.S. vegetable garden, with superb results, on our front lawn in a rather conservative suburb into which we had recently moved. This was early in World War II, and I think the neighborhood wrote me off as a mildly deranged British eccentric who had been reduced to horticultural absurdity because of the stress of the war! But since I had nowhere else in the entire yard where vegetables would thrive and I wanted to provide my young and growing family with plenty of fresh vegetables, I had no qualms about using a piece of grass where no one ever went because it was overlooked from the road. It took me a great many years to regrow a respectable lawn after that period was over. But to me the scruffy grass that followed the disappearance of the vegetables was far less attractive than the well-kept vegetable plot that had preceded it! Today no one worries nearly so much about any such unconventional behavior, and I have recently observed an increasing number of little plots smack in the middle of what once would have been considered sacred greensward. There are, however, some extra problems associated with growing vegetables near a road or street: fouling by dogs, air pollution, and roadside spraying by local authorities being the worst.

The best time to decide which is the right place in your yard is when the leaves of the trees are fully out and any neighboring houses are casting strong summer shadows. This means during the summer or early fall; winter and early spring **site prospecting** for a vegetable plot is less good. A leafless tree may seem quite harmless as you watch its shadow move around under the influence of the winter sun, but it may cast a much more serious, long-lasting shadow during the summer months, and not just because the tree has leafed out but because of the changed position of the sun. Obviously, not everyone can wait for high summer to plan for a future plot, so if you must decide during the winter months there are some basic rules to be followed.

Make very sure that your chosen garden plot is not immediately west or north of tall trees or big

buildings—that is to say, within 25 feet. Trees and buildings on the west side do not pose nearly such a serious shade problem, while any sort of protection to the north is a positive advantage, since this will protect the area from cold summer winds and from early frosts.

As a general rule keep a vegetable plot as far away as possible from established trees, particularly from any with shallow root systems. Tree roots will turn upward to take advantage of fertilizer and moisture and will always come out the winners in any struggle with the tender root systems of young vegetables. And, if you have any choice in the matter, choose a site sloping slightly down toward the south.

The best place for a vegetable garden is any spot that the family tends to avoid in the summer because it is too hot. The place where the experts have suggested that you put the family swimming pool is also usually the perfect position for vegetables! If you are really serious about raising your own edibles, this requirement for plenty of sunlight may call for some tree cutting and the removal of large shrubs. This is a hard matter of priorities, and only the individuals involved can make the decision, but for my personal taste, any yard without a single piece of open sunlit land is too shaded and dark.

Recently some newcomers moved into our summer village, and my first intimation that the house had changed hands was the sound of a chain saw and the sight of six or seven tall white pines being toppled. i found this sight and sound enormously discouraging. These were old, good trees, and I feared that their replacement was going to be a blacktop parking area. It turned out, however, that those trees were blocking the southern aspect of the only possible place to grow vegetables in that yard. The reluctant decision had been made to take them down before the new owner, who is a passionate organic gardener, could become attached to them. I am not sure how well the action set with the immediate neighbors, but the discovery that the trees had been felled to make way for a flourishing garden

put the picture in an entirely different perspective for me. I too had had to cut down a couple of large trees to make room for our present vegetable plot, and I could thoroughly sympathize with his dilemma. Unlike my new neighbor's, my tree cutting had been full of very personal regret. My trees were swamp maples that had given us years of pleasure with their flaming colors, and I greatly disliked deliberately destroying old friends that still had a good life span ahead. But for us a vegetable plot is essential to our complete enjoyment of the yard.

If you have to cut down trees there is, however, no need to force the yard to suffer visually forever. The abolished trees can be replaced with dwarf apple and peach trees; both begin cropping when young and can be set out in such a position that they neither steal goodness from the growing area nor throw any troublesome shade. This was the course followed by my new neighbor, and I now think his yard looks better with its thriving little fruit trees and flourishing vegetables than it did when the old pines dominated the scene.

If your land **slopes** slightly that is all to the good. Planted on the upper levels, tender crops will be far safer from unseasonably late or early frosts, for cold air flows downhill just like water. Any sort of elevated position for tender vegetables will prolong their growing period. Land at the top of a slope thaws out earlier than land at the bottom. This has the practical advantage of enabling you to start your spring work in one small area rather than having the entire growing space ready for action at the same exhausting moment. A steep slope presents more of a problem, and everyday gardening chores can soon take on the aspect of hard labor. Worse still, with a steep slope open soil tends to wash down in heavy rain, taking the seed with it and setting up a form of soil erosion. If you don't mind the effort involved in gardening on a steepish slope, you must remember to run the planting rows with the contour, that is, across the slope rather than up and down, in order to prevent soil washout. If your only possible position is a very steep slope you may have to consider terracing.

Rising ground in a garden presents other problems as well, for land at the bottom of a hill, the place where a child sliding

on a toboggan comes slowly to a halt, is also a poor place for vegetables. Vegetables are finicky about more than just getting plenty of sun. They also demand good **drainage** and good **air circulation,** and a low area in which water stands after a heavy rain will not suit them at all. If a low-lying, rather damp place is the only possible position for your vegetables, then the drainage problem can be largely eliminated by elevating the whole area by enclosing it with railway ties or treated 6-by-6-inch posts, thus turning it into something like a huge bin. This sort of **raised growing area** calls for a good deal of hard work and an enormous amount of extra soil, something new gardeners may have to buy at a considerable cost, but it is the only way to be sure of a harvest in a wet summer. Railway ties can be arranged to form the size you want, give a very neat appearance, and will generally last from ten to twenty years, depending on the amount of moisture in the area.

You can also, by adding soil, raise the level of growing areas for individual crops within your regular garden. These raised beds should be at least 15 inches across—24 inches would be better—and the soil must be packed down hard enough so that it does not wash away and can be safely raked over. You will need extra soil, preferably in the form of mulch and compost, to steadily renew any form of raised growing area, or the level will sink and the dampness of the ground seep through again.

If you don't mind the look, raised growing areas can also be made from cinderblocks laid end to end and butted very closely together to prevent soil from trickling through the joints. You can also stand cedar shakes against the inside of the concrete-block wall at each joint to insure against the soil's washing out. Laying the blocks should be done with a carpenter's level. If they are uneven in height the visual effect will be deplorable. Cinderblocks are practically impervious to decay, and they are reasonably light to handle. Using them makes the amount of area enclosed a much more·flexible affair than the use of railway ties. It is also a far less expensive way of enclosing raised areas. If they are set so that the open vents are upward, these holes can be filled with specially prepared soil

and used for certain heat-loving herbs that don't always do well in the rich growing soil needed to raise fine vegetables.

A disadvantage of raised beds is that they cannot be turned over by a rototiller if that is the way you intend to manage your soil. Also the long gulleys that lie between the raised beds are inclined to fill with standing water not only after a rainstorm but even after a good watering—and all raised areas dry out faster than level ground and therefore often need extra water. To have wet ground underfoot much of the time in a vegetable plot, even if it is not in the part where plants are growing, makes for uncomfortable working conditions.

Most vegetable gardens do best with some **protection** from the north, and if you garden by the sea or in a windy district, some general protection against wind will be necessary. Old-fashioned large vegetable gardens were sometimes enclosed by walls which served several purposes. They kept the utilitarian area out of sight, added to the warmth of the garden through reflected heat (something that made a huge difference in districts with a short growing season), deflected strong wind from any direction, and could be used as supports for climbing plants or fruit trees. They also kept the garden safe from many animals. But large, walled kitchen gardens, with enough interior space so that the wind crashed down on surrounding paths but not on growing areas, are not the sort of vegetable plot that we are considering, so what is the best modern equivalent that combines some of the virtues of the old walls? Nothing is quite as satisfactory as those walls, and there's no point pretending otherwise, but as a result of my experiences and what I have seen done by other vegetable gardeners I can give some kind of answer.

Our first vegetable plot on the suburban front lawn was protected from wind by the trees and shrubs along the boundary line that surrounded it on three sides at a distance of about 25 feet, while on the north the house provided protection. This kept the area safe from everything except the violent winds of a thunderstorm. Most vegetable plots that occupy front lawns will be equally well protected from wind by the neighboring community tree and shrub plantings. Since our children were

small at that time, we had the entire yard enclosed with a chain-link fence set deep into the shrubs along the boundary line, and the top of the drive was blocked with a gate which kept dogs out of the yard. That garden sloped a little upward from south to north, the perfect incline, and there was water to hand; it must, I think, count as the best-protected and best-sited of all my vegetable plots. It was also large enough, approximately 1,000 square feet, so that I could grow all the produce I needed.

If your garden is not so ideally sited I would suggest starting off by protecting a growing area with a simple wire-mesh fence. This **fencing,** which can be bought at lumber stores, can be held steady with special metal posts, with hooks welded onto metal pipes, or even with long stakes threaded through the mesh and driven deeply into the ground. As a precaution against the stakes' rotting, soak their bases in dirty crankcase oil for a couple of days before using them. This treatment preserves the wood and is much better than using any type of protective creosote, which is toxic to the soil and plants. Temporary fences put up this way do have a slightly unattractive habit of bulging and buckling, particularly if you try to train heavy plants such as tomatoes and cucumbers on them. If you are really interested in vegetable gardening, it is worthwhile having cedar fence posts and corner braces sunk along the sides of the plot and stapling the wire fencing to them. This will give a much sturdier fence; but don't forget to bury the base of the wire both to stabilize it and to serve as a mild deterrent to burrowing pests. For posts to stand really steady the holes must be at least 2 feet deep in coldest zones. **Digging post holes,** even with a special digger, is heavy work, but it can be done by amateurs. My husband and I put up the posts for an overhead trellis years ago when we were still pretty new to hard outdoor labor. We found it much easier to hold the posts steady if we backfilled the holes with all the big stones we could find before we filled in the open space with earth. A heavy iron rod with a pointed end can also be pounded into the ground and worked around with a circular motion to create a quick, efficient starter hole into which a fence post can be

pounded with a heavy mallet. If you can't imagine undertaking such a job, there are very attractive post and rail fences that can be put up professionally with wire stretched inside from post to post. This will not be cheap, but it will look very nice. A chain-link fence is another sturdy fencing alternative. If you have plenty of growing space surrounded in this manner, you can train climbing roses and clematis along one sunny side rather than dedicating all the upright growing space to climbing vegetables.

Any kind of fence, even a very amateurish type, will keep the growing area properly defined and look neat even when a heavy winter mulch is laid over the soil. The area at the base of the fence will become untidy and a haven for slugs and other plant pests if it is allowed to run to weeds and grass. A heavy mulch on both sides solves this problem. When snow fencing was common this made an excellent temporary fencing, though it was not too good for training climbing vegetables. It also took a lot of staking to hold it steady, but if you have some old rolls in storage use them as a starter. I am against string and plastic netting, even hooked into special metal posts. Netting does well for climbing plants in the growing area, but it is not strong enough to serve as fencing. Do not put a solid fence around a small vegetable plot. Solid fences cast shadows, and most plots can't take any extra shadows. Solid fences also resist wind instead of filtering it. As a result wind climbs up over the fence and crashes down on the other side about a foot away from the obstacle. A solid fence around a small plot causes more wind damage than no fence at all. Whatever kind of fence you decide upon, it is vital to make an opening large enough to get a big cart or tractor or rototiller through. Too small an entrance will give unending trouble. A gate will be much less of a nuisance if it is weighted with a ball and chain closure.

Gardeners who live in rural areas sometimes have to contend with inquisitive pasture animals. If there are cows, horses, or goats around, a low-voltage electric fence is the usual solution. The most useful kind has posts set about 12 feet apart with insulators set on the posts through which two strands of wire pass, one almost at ground level to jolt woodchucks and

rabbits, and the other about 3 feet from the ground. Power units (whether run by battery or by house current), posts, plastic insulators, and wire can be purchased for a modest price from any farm supply store. This is a case in which one should consult with a local farmer or someone who has set up this type of fence before. I have friends with electrified fences who swear by them, but they are obviously totally unsuitable for suburban gardening.

To sum up, a vegetable plot needs to be positioned where it has the most sun. It should be well drained and protected from the north. It should not have trees or big shrubs growing close against it, and it should be protected in some way from dogs and other animals. These are the first requirements.

Having found a possible place in a yard to grow vegetables, **just how large a plot should a new gardener take on**? And what is the minimum size that can produce a valuable return? In small suburban yards there may be very little leeway in this matter; the area given over to growing vegetables can only be as large as the space available.

Whether there is limited or extensive space, new gardeners would be wise not to think too big the first time around. Start off on a small scale that allows the cultivation of quite a lot of produce without producing boredom, exhaustion, and the "I-am-nothing-but-a-slave-to-the-garden" feelings that haunt those who've taken on more land than they have the time or the inclination or the ability to look after properly. Psychologically, it is always far better to feel annoyed by a crop limitation imposed upon you in a small garden and to plan to open up more land next season than to be defeated by a weed-filled, nonproductive, large garden. Few of us are ever willing to reduce the size of a plot if we fail; we're far more likely to give up growing vegetables altogether. This, incidentally, is one of the reasons why a permanent fence should not be put around a growing area until a couple of experimental years have passed. Without practical experience, it is almost impossible to know in advance what will prove manageable or too large for you. It also takes time to decide whether you want to grow only what your family will consume during the coming grow-

ing season, or whether you will have time and inclination to process surplus crops for later use.

The style in which you decide to garden (open soil, which has to be kept weeded, or mulched land, for which mulching material must be found) also needs to be determined through firsthand experience. The fact that it is perfectly possible to grow certain vegetables in containers in a sunny place, and not necessarily in a garden plot, is another reason for being rather cautious. It's not a bad idea for those completely new to vegetable growing to start with a few container vegetables (pages 124–32) before they undertake anything else—to get the feel of planning for and harvesting an edible crop.

About the smallest size that will bring a worthwhile return is something around 100 square feet. A square plot 10 feet by 10 feet, or a long, oblong bed 6 feet by 16 feet, is a possible

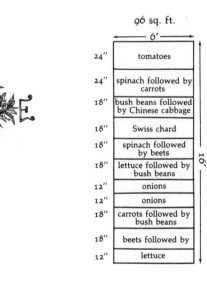

96 sq. ft.

	6'	
24"	tomatoes	
24"	spinach followed by carrots	
18"	bush beans followed by Chinese cabbage	
18"	Swiss chard	
18"	spinach followed by beets	16'
18"	lettuce followed by bush beans	
12"	onions	
12"	onions	
18"	carrots followed by bush beans	
18"	beets followed by	
12"	lettuce	

A plot of approximately 100 square feet could contain four staked tomatoes, successive rows of various varieties of loose-leaf lettuce for spring and fall, successive rows of bush beans, beets, and carrots, one all-season row of Swiss chard, two rows of onions from sets, two rows of early spinach, a row of fall Chinese cabbage, together with radishes and clump plantings of basil, dill, garlic, chives, parsley, and tarragon around the edges of the plot.

idea. The long, narrow bed has some advantages for the complete novice. The 6-foot width allows it to be worked from both sides, without having to be walked on and compacting the soil. Also, a 6-foot row of almost any crop is usually enough for an average family when it all comes to harvest at much the same moment.

For those who find it hard to visualize size in terms of square footage, among whom I count myself, it is a help to find a rug that has approximately the same dimensions, 10 by 10. Seeing a potential plot spread out on the floor brings everything into much sharper focus. If you have no such rug, mark out a space on a floor with chalk or tape, anything that will give a strong outline. Just as an empty room in a house never looks as though it can contain the furniture you mean to put into it, so will the space laid out on your floor seem absurdly small. Nevertheless, it helps a great deal to stare at it and then plot it on a piece of paper, indicating the crops that your family likes and that you hope you will be able to get into this space.

Since most of the recommendations for fertilizers are given in relation to an area of 100 square feet, it makes sense in this discussion to stick to this unit when we are dealing with the size of possible growing areas. A plot twice as large as the smallest practical size, that is up to 200 square feet, will not be able to take very many other types of vegetables than the original small area. If the gardener expands his plot three or four times as large, that is, up to 300 or 400 square feet, which is, incidentally, quite large enough for any beginning gardener, then it is possible to include a good many other vegetables that cannot be grown in the small plot. My present vegetable garden, which I put in after the family grew up and left home, is a little less than 400 square feet. It's not too large for me to handle alone, nor is it too large to be kept under perpetual mulch, which is very important to my style of gardening.

Once you've reached the size of 400 square feet, it is important to bisect the growing area with paths. In my plot I have a single path running through the center. It is much easier, both for novice and for experienced gardeners, to work in small, defined areas, compartmentalized within the main growing

408 sq. ft.

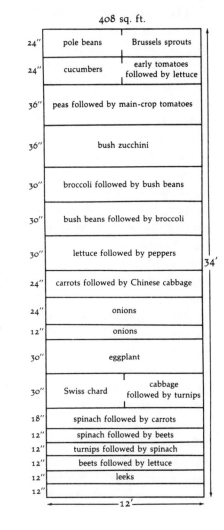

24"	pole beans / Brussels sprouts
24"	cucumbers / early tomatoes followed by lettuce
36"	peas followed by main-crop tomatoes
36"	bush zucchini
30"	broccoli followed by bush beans
30"	bush beans followed by broccoli
30"	lettuce followed by peppers
24"	carrots followed by Chinese cabbage
24"	onions
12"	onions
30"	eggplant
30"	Swiss chard / cabbage followed by turnips
18"	spinach followed by carrots
12"	spinach followed by beets
12"	turnips followed by spinach
12"	beets followed by lettuce
12"	leeks
12"	

34'

12'

A plot of approximately 400 square feet could have all the same vegetables as the 100-square-foot plot, except that it could have both early and main-crop tomatoes staked, probably three early and six late. It could also have broccoli, early cabbage, fall Brussels sprouts, bush zucchini, eggplant, sweet peppers, cucumbers grown on a trellis, turnips, and leeks, if they happen to be to your taste.

space, than to try to tackle a huge open area. Compartments within a vegetable garden also make it easier to limit the length of a furrow of any one seed that is planted or plants that are set out. The paths need not be elaborate or even permanent. All that is needed is something to set apart their limits from the growing area. Some gardeners define the limits of their paths by pegging in boards, and this makes a very neat-appearing garden. The surface of the paths can be made by piling bark mulch over the open ground, or by spreading tarpaper, or, which is the way I do it, by laying down a permanent path of cement blocks, butted closely together in a layer of sand. But whatever the surface, it should always be wide enough to accommodate a garden cart. Being able to bring supplies in a barrow or a cart close to the spot where you are working greatly diminishes the labor involved.

From this 400 square feet of garden, I am able to feed a family of three with plenty of vegetables throughout the growing season, and we are voracious vegetable eaters. I do not have any surplus to can. I grow all the vegetables we need in it— except peas, corn, and potatoes—together with a certain number of basic herbs. I now raise tomatoes, pole beans, and cucumbers elsewhere in the yard, for I need space in the plot for some experimental work. I have in the past, however, raised all three crops with great success on trellises within the plot, and had more than enough room to spare for everything else.

When the family was much larger and we fed seven people daily, the old vegetable plot was twice as large, almost 800 square feet. In those days, I neither mulched nor practiced succession cultivation, but even so I had no problem at all in keeping the family supplied throughout the growing season.

A plot of approximately 1,000 square feet, which should produce plenty of surplus crops, could have all the same vegetables as the 100- and 400-square-foot plots, and, in addition, it could have fall cauliflower, early, late, and red cabbage, parsnips, kale, corn, melon, vining squash in variety, and two big perennial crops, a double row of asparagus, and some clumps of rhubarb.

1,000 sq. ft.

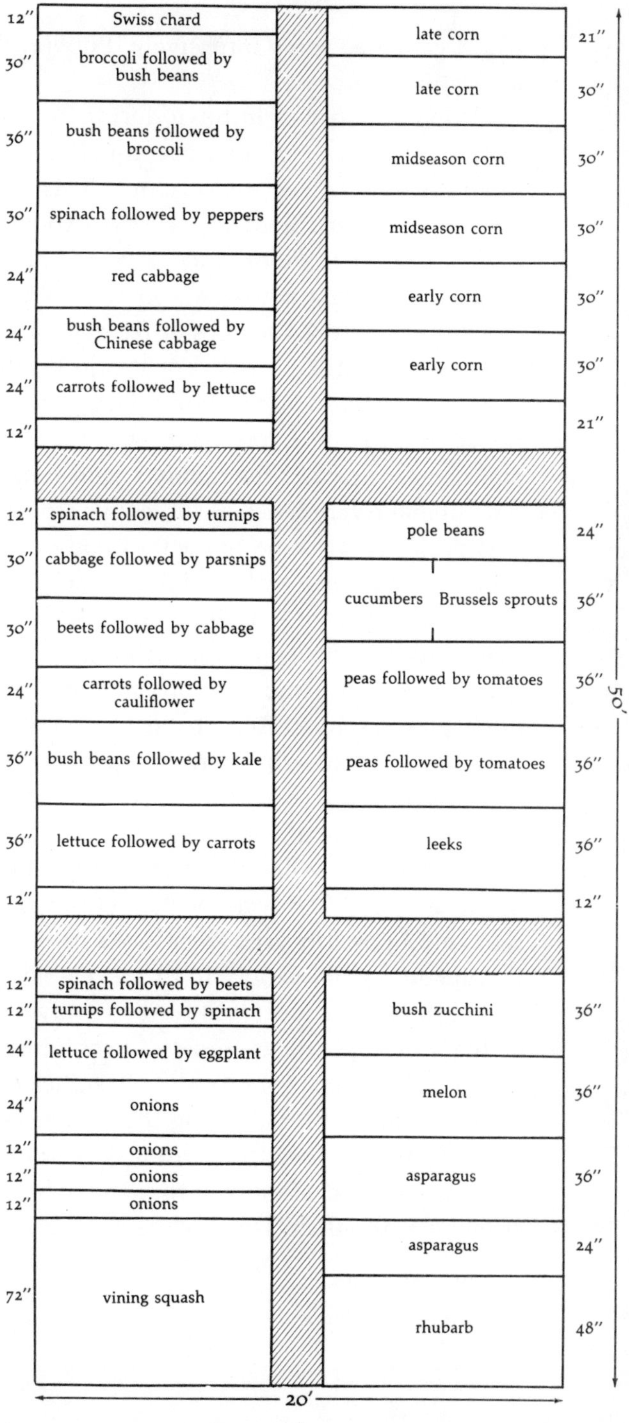
12″ Swiss chard
30″ broccoli followed by bush beans
36″ bush beans followed by broccoli
30″ spinach followed by peppers
24″ red cabbage
24″ bush beans followed by Chinese cabbage
24″ carrots followed by lettuce
12″
late corn 21″
late corn 30″
midseason corn 30″
midseason corn 30″
early corn 30″
early corn 30″
21″
12″ spinach followed by turnips
30″ cabbage followed by parsnips
30″ beets followed by cabbage
24″ carrots followed by cauliflower
36″ bush beans followed by kale
36″ lettuce followed by carrots
12″
pole beans 24″
cucumbers Brussels sprouts 36″
peas followed by tomatoes 36″
peas followed by tomatoes 36″
leeks 36″
12″
12″ spinach followed by beets
12″ turnips followed by spinach
24″ lettuce followed by eggplant
24″ onions
12″ onions
12″ onions
12″ onions
72″ vining squash
bush zucchini 36″
melon 36″
asparagus 36″
asparagus 24″
rhubarb 48″
50′
20′

Had I gardened more intensively, I obviously could have had a surplus to process.

When I gardened in town during World War II, I worked an area that was around 1,000 square feet. There I gardened intensively with successive crops. This, as I've already described, was a particularly well situated site, and it produced a great deal of spare produce. I canned and stored vegetables in gleaming glass containers in the cold cellar, for this, of course, was before the days of freezers in every house. When the government, at the start of World War II, was urging victory gardens upon homeowners, it suggested a size of 30 by 50 feet; that is to say, 1,500 square feet, as being suitable "to grow an important part of the family's food supply." The pamphlet did not make very much of successive cropping. In my opinion, it is perfectly possible to feed a family of four, with surplus produce available, with a plot that ranges from about 1,000 square feet upward. I have two friends who have a plot a little over 1,400 square feet who, without successive planting and with an enormous number of summer visitors all hungry for home produce, processed a large number of vegetables, enough to make a considerable dent in their food bills.

To sum up, it would seem sensible for a brand-new gardener to start with a small garden, 10 by 10, or two similar-sized plots. This will only fractionally cut down on the green produce you must buy at the market (it would be a rare family that could possibly feed themselves on so small a space), but it will add a great variety to the vegetables you eat. A plot of 300 to 400 square feet will feed a family of four, and if some of the vining plants are grown in containers, it may enable a family to be almost completely self-sufficient where vegetables are concerned, at least during the summer growing season. A fairly large plot, anything from 800 square feet upward, is necessary to feed a family of four and to have sufficient surplus crops to make them worthwhile processing for the winter.

Soil

Another enormously important part of growing vegetables is the soil in which you expect to raise them. Good topsoil for vegetables is deep, rich, and light. It is full of air but with a slightly coarse texture; overfine soil is not good growing soil. Good soil is normally dark, free of stones, and absorbs water easily, but it should not hold water so long that it becomes sodden. To be rich it must contain a full supply of the various mineral and trace elements that all growing things need to thrive, and, of particular importance in small plots where a succession of crops is planned, this supply of nutrients and trace elements must exist in sufficient amounts to be present not only at the start of the season but throughout the growing months.

These are demanding requirements that few garden soils can meet unaided, and they are just as vital as the need for sunlight. The reason why the condition of the soil does not come first on my list of essentials for success with vegetables is that a great deal can be done to improve home soil, whereas up to the present, nothing can be done, short of cutting down trees, to improve outdoor sunlight where that is lacking! Soil and soil fertility are immensely complicated subjects that I shall have to oversimplify. But even in this compressed account, it must be stressed that the key to long-term success in

vegetable growing lies in understanding what soil is and how it works to help plants grow.

Occasionally by chance and with some help from that rare double play, good luck and good weather, a novice gardener will grow a fine crop of vegetables on a piece of ground to which he has done nothing at all other than some light digging —if that. Because this can happen, some people think that too much is made by the so-called gardening experts of the importance of soil conditioning. There also exist worry warts who take the reverse attitude that a tremendous amount must always be done all the time in the way of artificial aids. As usual, the truth lies somewhere in the middle of these two extremes.

I used to belong to the group who, after an initial success with vegetables on unimproved land, felt that far too much fuss is made about good soil. My front lawn vegetable extravaganza was planted without any particular attention to the soil other than a quick raking to get the stones out of the area from which I had just stripped the sod. What's more, it did beautifully—for a couple of years. But then the day of reckoning arrived. The crops became spindly and diseased, they turned a poor color, and bugs that I had never seen previously in the yard appeared. By the fourth season the crop return was not worth the effort I put into the plot. What had happened became painfully clear. I had made that garden on rich, deep topsoil that had once been part of an old orchard, land that had been well treated in the past. When I reopened it for cultivation there were still sufficient minerals in the soil, and the soil structure was still good enough to produce fine vegetables with virtually no help from me. But, after two years, the fertility was depleted and the soil became overfine from constant cultivating. The plants also had taken a great deal of the nutrient content out of the soil, without anything having been put back or brought up from below. So my vegetables were starved, became stunted and weak, and an open invitation both to disease and to attack by all kinds of bugs. Unhealthy vegetables are far more likely to attract pests than strongly growing specimens. The poor colors that showed up in the foliage were also an exact indication of the mineral deficiencies that by now existed in the soil.

Broccoli

If you want to go ahead and plant a vegetable plot in your soil just as it is, with no extra effort, you may or may not get a good crop. But if you intend to grow vegetables for many years on the same piece of land it is extremely important to understand the formation of soil and how it promotes good growth. Without this understanding your later crops on unimproved soil will be a certain failure. Keeping the soil of a vegetable or a flower garden in fine growing condition for many consecutive years is not a complicated or necessarily expensive business; what is required is a little specific knowledge and the will to translate this knowledge into action, faithfully and regularly.

If you could look down into one of those enormous holes that are dug for the foundations of skyscrapers, you would see three very distinctive layers of soil. At the very lowest level there is **bedrock,** the geological stratum on which all loose soil rests. Bedrock can be igneous, that is formed through heat, or sedimentary, laid down by water, and these two basic formations are divided up into many different geological manifestations. Different types of bedrock contain differing amounts of mineral deposits as well as trace elements, so the mineral riches in bedrock can vary tremendously from place to place. Above the bedrock rise huge deposits of **subsoil**. Subsoil is formed from the weathering through natural forces of the bedrock beneath, so subsoil will contain exactly the same ratio of mineral and trace elements as the underlying rock stratum. During the most ancient periods of earth's history when bedrock was being formed, the sedimentary bedrock, that laid by water, was organic—it contained life. But during the millions of years that have passed since it was laid down, all traces of bacterial life in the forms of microorganisms have long since vanished from it, and today all bedrock and the subsoil formed from it count as inorganic material—something that contains absolutely no forms of life or any organic matter.

The third and uppermost layer of the earth's crust is composed of **topsoil,** which is a totally different substance from either bedrock or subsoil. Topsoil is formed from the decomposition by soil organisms of organic matter that accumulates

on the surface of the ground. Anything that once lived, dead weeds and grass, leaves, fallen trees and broken branches, animal droppings and animal carcasses and any solid object made from a once-living material will, if given time, plenty of oxygen, and the availability of moisture, be broken down or decomposed by soil organisms into loose, rich humus. The depth of this layer and its fertility is the crux of good plant growth; for in topsoil, and for the most part only in topsoil, plants spread their roots and take in the nourishment that they must have to live.

Topsoil draws an important part of its fertility, its nitrogen, from the organic materials from which it was originally formed and from the atmosphere. Other mineral and trace elements also rise into it from the subsoil. This happens when there is an exchange, an intermingling of subsoil and topsoil, something that can occur as a result of abnormal weather or water conditions, from the action of burrowing animals, or through the deliberate intervention of man.

A layer of topsoil exists everywhere, though in very rocky or very dry areas it can be pitifully thin and able to support the root systems of only small top growth. In river and mountain valleys, in alluvial plains, or in forested areas the layer of topsoil can run very deep and grow lush vegetation and trees. One of the first jobs to be undertaken by a gardener, whether he intends to grow ornamental plants or vegetables, or is beginning to think about landscaping his ground, is to dig a hole and find out how deep he has to go before the spade hits the harder, lighter-colored, more densely packed subsoil. If there is a very small layer of topsoil, a matter of only a few inches, it will be necessary to increase this organic layer. But even if the loose top layer seems to run deep, it does not follow that it is good growing soil: the physical structure may be poor, and essential nutritional elements may be missing or may be there but held under conditions in which the plants' roots can make no use of them. For though topsoil is totally different in origin from the layers of subsoil and bedrock that lie beneath it, the physical structure of topsoil is nevertheless controlled by this buried inorganic material.

Subsoil has been created by the slow wearing down or abrasion of the underlying bedrock. The abraded rock breaks up in two ways, according to the basic geology of the rocks themselves. One type of rock formation produces subsoil which consists (in microscopic form) of large jagged particles which combine loosely together and allow water to pass swiftly through. When this loosely linked subsoil meets and mingles with the layer of topsoil that lies over it, it is easily penetrated by air particles that form tiny oxygen-filled pockets around each individual particle of soil. Subsoil with these characteristics produces what we call a **sandy topsoil.** Other bedrock formations break up into microscopically tiny particles that cling tightly together. In this type of subsoil water penetrates very slowly and passes through extremely reluctantly. And where these tightly knit particles of subsoil come into contact with the topsoil, air also finds it hard to get in. Topsoil affected by this form of subsoil becomes a **clay soil.**

Air in the soil is immensely important for good plant growth. The oxygen air contains is used in the chemical process that converts soil minerals into the water-soluble mineral solutions that plants absorb through their root hairs—those tiny feathery rootlings on the tip end of every root. Plants also absorb pure oxygen itself as part of their growth process, so airless, closely packed soil cannot grow good plants. Most of us have seen protective measures being taken to provide plants with vital air around their roots without quite understanding what is going on. Golf greens that get constantly trampled upon become compacted—that is, the air is driven out from the pressure of countless feet concentrated on a small area. Those spiking machines that can be seen working over golf greens are punching holes to let in air. When building or buying a house it is important to understand this principle. Heavy building machines crisscrossing an area can compact the soil fatally. Always be certain that the area where you want to garden has been completely protected not only from machinery but also from piles of concrete blocks and bricks. For these too compact soil by their weight if they are left there too long.

All soil in the United States is basically either sandy or

clayey or some combination between the two extremes. Knowing which type exists in your yard is extremely important. It will govern the way you improve your soil, and the time when you carry out this improvement. It makes a difference in the period when you plant and the best way to do so. It will also give you a better understanding of how weather is likely to affect a vegetable crop and what precautions you must take about where you put your feet when working in the yard!

The simple way to identify your particular type of soil is to take a dampened handful of topsoil and rub it through your fingers. Sandy soil will feel sharp and gritty and will leave the skin of your fingers in need of soothing hand lotion. Clay soil will be sticky, and the heavier the clay content, the greater the difficulty you will have rubbing it off. Loamy soil, a happy combination of the two extremes that few of us have naturally in our yards, will glide in a silken fashion through your fingers a little like well-oiled dough.

Bedrock and subsoil exert other important influences on that vital organic layer of topsoil, for these underlying geological formations also control the acid/alkaline balance of the topsoil (see page 31), and the minerals and trace elements that were contained in the original bedrock make a great difference to topsoil fertility. Some bedrock formations are much richer in soil minerals than others, and this disparity naturally shows up in the subsoil and eventually in the topsoil.

This, then, is the natural manner in which varying depths and different mineral wealth affect the amount and quality of the topsoil and give it differing physical characteristics. But few places where we live are now as they were originally. Except in rare instances, most of us live where man has also long been present, and where man has been around, the natural evolutionary processes in which the layers of the earth's crust are laid down get radically altered.

If, like me and my first vegetable plot, you garden in an area that was once farm land, the layer of topsoil is likely to have been artificially deepened. That garden of mine lay in a pocket among rock ledges that rise almost to the surface, and on what remains of those ledges there is very little topsoil. But this was

sunny land that sloped southward down to a pond, ideal for fruit growing, and the farmers who worked it must have deliberately broken up the rock ledges, presumably with fire, water, and crowbars, and hauled away tons of rocks and stones in order to get it plowed and planted to apple trees. And when they plowed, these farmers clearly went deliberately each time a small distance into the subsoil in order to break that up and let air in. Presumably they incorporated organic matter, probably animal manures, into the disturbed subsoil and thus increased the depth of the layer containing organic matter to help their trees grow. There is no other way to explain the depth of topsoil in this rocky, hilly slope of land, and what happened here must have occurred all across the eastern seaboard wherever farmers had to try to wring a living out of soil that was, in fact, naturally too shallow to grow good crops.

Another way in which man alters the natural pattern of the land is by filling, that is adding soil. This is done to marshy or sunken areas to raise them above the water table. Other forms of fills are old dumps, mine tailings, and soil thrown into abandoned quarries to make them suitable for housing developments. Marshy land that has been filled usually has a considerable depth of so-called topsoil; old dumps, tailings, and quarry land usually contain only a small skim of artificially added topsoil. Fill is almost always of very poor quality, usually composed of subsoil that has been taken out of some other excavated area. Land under development in what was once wooded area sometimes, rather astonishingly, proves to have only an inch or so of topsoil. Such land should have deep topsoil laid down over the years by the decaying leaves from the original tree cover. But deep, natural topsoil is a valuable commodity, and unscrupulous contractors often scrape it off and sell it. A wretched skim of mixed topsoil and subsoil from somewhere else is spread over the stripped land and left to serve as the growing layer for the unwitting new owner.

All these possible combinations of circumstances make it very hard to judge offhand, if you are new to gardening, anything more than the extent of the layer of topsoil in your yard and whether it is sandy or clayey. What's more, this first inves-

tigation may prove rather horrifying, for you may well find very little topsoil and what does exist in very poor, stony condition. Or it may be hard clay, so crusted that you can hardly break through. But, very fortunately,

with soil all is never lost, no matter how wretched your growing layer may appear to be. If you will take some simple steps even the worst-looking layer can, in time, be converted into excellent soil, and with forethought, you can get some immediate return for your efforts in the very first season.

To be productive, that is, grow good crops year after year, soil must meet certain specifications. It must have a correct acid/alkaline balance, usually expressed in the form of a pH scale. It has to contain the mineral and trace elements plants need to have to thrive, and it must continue to manufacture these elements with your assistance as long as you are taking heavy crops out of it. It must hold water neither so long, if it is clay soil, nor for so short a time, if it is sandy soil, that plant roots cannot make proper use of the soil moisture and the minerals it contains. These are vital and basic requirements, and any one of them seriously out of kilter can ruin plant growth. But fortunately, once they are identified almost all of these factors can be corrected without too much effort; problems arise only when the soil weaknesses are not identified and properly handled.

The **acid/alkaline or pH balance** is a term that frightens many gardeners so much that they put off trying to understand it, and ignorance on this matter can lead to serious growing problems. All soil, to varying degrees, is either acid (sour) or alkaline (sweet); neutral soil with an exact balance between the two is very rare and occurs mostly in the Mediterranean area. Soil gets this way mainly through the geological makeup of the underlying bedrock, but climate also plays a part. Wet areas tend to have an acid soil, dry climates an alkaline soil. The reason the degree of acidity or alkalinity in the subsoil and topsoil matters is because high levels either way affect the availability of the food elements in the topsoil. At certain

levels on the pH scale these nutrients, whether they occur naturally in the soil or have been added by the gardener, can be converted quickly into water-soluble minerals that plant roots can absorb. At extreme levels these nutrients become insoluble (cannot dissolve into the soil water), so their goodness is locked up and wasted. Some of the trace elements that are also essential for good plant growth turn toxic at extreme pH levels and damage the plants instead of helping them. So though a gardener can have, either through the bounty of nature or through additives, every element in the soil that plants need, if the pH is extreme in either direction nothing will grow well. The situation could perhaps be compared to eating a perfectly balanced nutritious meal but running such a high or subnormal fever that the system can neither absorb the food nor keep it down.

Main Elements and Trace Elements
Main elements: Nitrogen (N)
   Phosphorus or phosphate (P_2O_5)
   Potash (K_2O)
Trace elements: Iron

Boron	Copper
Manganese	Molybdenum
Zinc	Chlorine

(also calcium and magnesium that are derived from soil minerals or from limestone applications)

So what does this all-important pH scale look like, and what are the dangerous readings? A pH scale can be thought of as a fever thermometer with fourteen readings, normal, or neutral as it is called, being 7.0. Continuing the fever analogy, acid soil has "subnormal" readings, intensely acid soil showing a reading of 4.5 on the pH scale. Alkaline soil reaction starts

above the "normal" 7.0 mark, 8.0 being extremely alkaline.

Most plants flourish and get the most out of the nutrients and trace elements in the soil under slightly acidic conditions, around the 6.5 mark.

Vegetables prefer a soil that lies within the 6.5 to 7.0 range, but they will grow with a pH reading as low as 5.4. Aromatic edible herbs do best with a slightly sweeter soil, a reading around the 7.0 mark.

For generations gardeners raised excellent plants without knowing the acid/alkaline reactions of their soils in any exact detail. They observed what grew well wild in the neighborhood and what did well in their yards, and they chose their plants accordingly. They also judged the fertility of their land by the look of their plants. But this style of gardening, flying by the seat of the pants, calls for a great deal of practical experience and also a willingness to grow vegetables on a trial basis the first time.

Today there is no need to wait a full growing season to discover how well your garden grows and then guess at what you should do. **Soil testing** takes away the guesswork, for it gives you the pH reading for your soil as well as the ratio of nitrogen, phosphorus, and potash it contains.

There are two ways soil can be tested. It can be done professionally, sometimes for free and sometimes for a small fee from a county or state extension service or agricultural station: look in the yellow pages of the telephone book for the listings under your state. Professional testing takes time; in the spring and early summer the wait can be as long as six weeks, which can be extremely frustrating and leads most people into going ahead without waiting for the results. It is better to send a sample to be tested in the fall. The extension services are much less busy at that time, and the results will come faster. And fall is by far the best time to do any necessary work on garden soil. The information when it comes back will often be based on very large acreage and not seem suitable for small garden plots. The chart on page 34 shows a rough conversion table by which you can adjust their recommendations for your size plot.

Fertilizing in Small Gardens

Amateur gardeners are often puzzled regarding the amount of fertilizer to use on their small plots, because the customary directions give only the amount per acre. The following table shows (approximately) the proper proportions:

100 lb. per acre equals 1 lb. for a plot 10 by 43 ft. (430 sq. ft.)
200 lb. per acre equals 1 lb. for a plot 10 by 21 ft. (210 sq. ft.)
300 lb. per acre equals 1 lb. for a plot 10 by 14 ft. (140 sq. ft.)
400 lb. per acre equals 1 lb. for a plot 10 by 11 ft. (110 sq. ft.)
500 lb. per acre equals 1 lb. for a plot 10 by 9 ft. (90 sq. ft.)

The standard application for a balanced plant food is 3 to 5 pounds per 100 square feet (a space 10 by 10 feet square). You may figure one pound per pint, so an area 10 by 10 feet requires 1½ to 2½ quarts. One quart will feed 50 square feet and one pint 25 square feet. Where small quantities are required, use a rounded tablespoon per square foot. For convenience, here is a table showing some common areas and the standard balanced plant food application for each:

5 ft. by 5 ft. equals   25 sq. ft.—requires   1 lb. (or 1 pt.)
5 ft. by 10 ft. equals   50 sq. ft.—requires   2 lb. (or 1 qt.)
10 ft. by 10 ft. equals 100 sq. ft.—requires   4 lb. (or 2 qt.)
20 ft. by 30 ft. equals 600 sq. ft.—requires 24 lb.
25 ft. by 100 ft. equals 2,500 sq. ft.—requires 100 lb.

—Courtesy of *Horticulture*

The other way to test soil is to do it at home with one of the many excellent testing kits that are available at hardware stores and garden centers. I would avoid the very cheap types that test by means of litmus strips. Get a kit that tests with chemicals; this will give much more accurate readings. Buy your kit locally; don't send away for one. Not all kits are formulated in a manner that suits every type of soil; your local store will carry the kits that work properly in your area. None of these kits is hard to use. All you need do is follow the instructions, and there is a great deal of useful additional information incorporated into these instruction sheets. I am greatly in favor of home testing; you get a quick answer and the kits have enough of the necessary materials for several tests, which is important.

Soil samples for testing are always collected the same way. Use a clean trowel and dig up samples of soil at random from your plot in three or four places about 2 inches below the soil surface. Soil is taken below surface level to avoid casual contamination. Plaster from old walls would, for example, completely change the pH reading of a sample. The clean trowel is to avoid bringing soil in from some other area, and your hands should not touch the samples, since sweat from them is also a contaminant. Drop the samples into a plastic bag and shake them up well; then scoop out a cupful, put that into another plastic bag, and send it off. If you are home testing, leave the samples unsullied in the original bag until you have completely understood the instructions that will be in the kit.

If the **pH reading** in the plot proves too acid for vegetables —that is, well below the 6.0 mark—ground agricultural limestone, or lime, will raise the pH level, or "sweeten the soil," as old gardeners used to say.

> **To raise the pH a point in clay soils 5 pounds of limestone will be needed for each 100 square feet; with sandy soils half that amount will do. To decrease the pH use 2 pounds of agricultural sulfur or ferrous sulfate for every 100 square feet of clay soil and 1 pound in sandy soil.**

The slightly more expensive dolomite limestone is the best you can use. Dolomitic or ground limestone can be used in combination with whatever extra fertilizer the tests show the soil needs, but if you buy hydrated lime, which does just as good a job at bringing up the pH of overacid soil, you cannot combine it with fertilizers or manure, for it will react chemically with them. With hydrated lime, two weeks must pass before adding fertilizers of any kind. If the soil test shows a high alkaline reading, agricultural sulfur or ferrous sulfate will bring down the pH level.

Limestone used to be a gardener's cure-all, and it was used heavily and automatically every year on both the lawns and the vegetable garden in my father's and my grandfather's garden. Looking back I wonder if quite so much was really needed, but since both those gardens were on very sticky clay its use was probably justified, not so much to sweeten the soil as to break it up. For limestone incorporated into clay soils in the fall (which is the only time of year clay soil should be dug) improves the physical texture of the clay and not only makes it easier to work but also opens it up for better root penetration in the spring. Limestone is the best and most inexpensive soil conditioner around if it is needed, but the key words here are "if it is needed." For as we have already seen, too much lime can lock up essential nutrients even though it may improve the soil structure, and that is the reason why a proper test for pH is so vitally important before lime is spread annually and automatically.

The next matter is, of course, the question of **soil fertility:** where does it come from, how to find out if there is an adequate supply, how best is it added to soils, in what quantity and at what season? Soil to deserve the term fertile has to be able to supply plants with a great number of different elements over a full growing season. Of the big three elements, nitrogen, phosphorus, and potash (sometimes called NPK), **nitrogen** exists only in the topsoil; there is none in the subsoil. Nitrogen comes from the air. It does not exist in a mineral form, and it is produced in the topsoil through the actions of special soil bacteria as they break down organic matter (the dead plant and

animal material that either collects naturally upon the soil's surface or is added to the topsoil or piled upon it by the gardener). The nitrogen in the air is also introduced into the topsoil by bacteria in a process known as nitrogen fixation. The nitrogen that is introduced into the soil by these two methods has to go through a complicated chemical sequence in order to become available in a form that plant roots can absorb. Earthworms add this absorbable nitrogen to the topsoil, for their castings are rich in nitrates, which is the form in which roots absorb that vital element. Plenty of nitrogen in the topsoil brings strong leafy growth. All plants need nitrogen, but in vegetable gardening the plants that we eat for their leaves—lettuce, spinach, chard, kale, and all "greens"—need the most for quick succulent growth.

Phosphorus is also produced through the decomposition of organic matter. It exists in mineral form in the bedrock and subsoil and thus rises into the topsoil. It encourages early flowering and heavy cropping, so its presence in sufficient quantity in a vegetable plot is of great importance for such plants as tomatoes, peppers, and eggplants. All plants and vegetables will suffer, showing stunted growth, if there is a deficiency of phosphorus.

Potash, or potassium, as it is sometimes called, is also a natural mineral in the soil and acts as a sort of catalyst that helps the plants absorb the other two elements. Potash encourages vigorous root growth, and its availability appears to be a factor that affects the hardiness of plants. If you burn a wood fire, wood ashes, which are full of potash, make an excellent top dressing for any vegetable garden early in the spring. But the goodness of wood ash leaches away extremely fast when it is wet, so surplus wood ash should always be stored under cover and made available to plant roots when they are ready to use it. It should not be used in the preparation of the ground in the fall.

By law, all bags of fertilizer must have written on them the proportion of nitrogen, phosphorus, and potash they contain. This ratio is shown by three numbers such as 5-10-5: the first 5 represents the nitrogen content; the 10, the phosphorus; and

the final 5, the potash. The point of the numerals is to enable you to match up the particular needs of your soil with the right fertilizer.

Fall Fertilizing

As a general rule, if you are getting your ground ready in the fall or winter, choose a fertilizer high in phosphorus and potash, something in the nature of 5-10-5, or better still 5-20-10, and apply it, together with lime (if needed) and organic matter, at the rate of 5 pounds per 100 square feet.

A high nitrogen-count fertilizer should not be added in the winter, because nitrogen is an unstable element that tends to leach out before the growing season arrives. Any small amount you add in the fall, together with the new amount that will be produced through decomposition of organic matter, will suffice for the very early stages of the next season's growth. When the leafy plants are well above ground, then is the time to add extra nitrogen.

Fertilizers come in two types: those made from chemicals and those that are organic or natural in origin. Recently there has been a great deal of controversy about which should be used. I feel as strongly as anyone about the damage that has been done to our environment through the overuse of certain chemical fertilizers, but this argument does not really apply to small vegetable plots. And there are some other aspects of the organic/chemical controversy that are not always recognized. Even in these days of soaring prices, chemical fertilizers are still much cheaper than the organic varieties. If we are gardening to cut down on the food bills that is something to bear in mind. They also work much faster, and much less is needed. Where

five pounds of chemical fertilizer is called for, ten pounds of organic fertilizer would be needed. The speed with which chemical fertilizers go to work seems to me to be another very important aspect of home vegetable growing. New gardeners need to be encouraged by seeing quick results. All too easily new gardeners can be turned off by hot, hard work that doesn't produce visible results.

The argument that there is a different quality to the food elements provided by organic and chemical fertilizers does not really stand up. Nothing we add to the land is taken up by the roots in the form in which we put it in; it all has to undergo a chemical change that makes it water-soluble. Once in water solution there is no difference between the mineral elements provided by chemical and organic fertilizers. Where chemical fertilizers do lose out is in improving the quality of the soil. Other than the minerals they contain, they are inert. Organic fertilizers, on the other hand, contain soil bacteria which turn immediately to work improving the topsoil by decomposing organic matter. For new gardeners just opening up their first plot, I would suggest using chemical fertilizer. In subsequent years, if you garden my way, there will be far less need for any

Parsnips

store-bought fertilizer, and that's the time to choose the slow-er-acting organic materials that will build up the soil as they add to its fertility.

As the term **organic matter** has arisen at every stage in this discussion, it must be very obvious that it is one of the essential products that must be added to soil. A large quantity of organic matter is absolutely essential in vegetable plots for good soil structure and for its fertility. Mechanically, organic matter will serve as a sponge and hold moisture long enough for the roots to make use of the minerals that dissolve into it. In clay soils, organic matter breaks apart the closely knit clay particles and makes it easier for stagnant water to drain out. Where soil fertility is involved, organic matter is the key substance. When there is plenty of it either in the layer of topsoil or laid on top of it, there will be millions of soil bacteria hard at work. And where millions of bacteria are at work there will be plenty of essential nutrients available for the plant roots. Soil bacteria work fast; it takes them and the worms they attract a relatively short time to break down rough or coarse organic material into fine black humus. Soil bacteria always exist in the topsoil, though in a less active form than when fresh organic matter is present. But to keep a steady supply of these essential and ravenous bacteria at work, organic matter must be regularly added to every vegetable plot. In the next chapter, I will discuss how a new gardener finds this black gold, and how he can make it for himself in subsequent years.

Organic
Matter

 Organic matter is obviously the hero of any soil improvement scheme for both immediate and long-term results. Owners of vegetable plots who don't want to make this essential material at home must be prepared to put up with the cost of buying it, which is going to make the vegetable garden almost as expensive as the produce stall at the supermarket! Since I do not consider anyone a real gardener unless he is prepared to build up his own supply of organic matter by saving plant wastes, I don't have much sympathy for people who continuously complain about the price of organic substitutes that must be used if their ground is to grow fine crops. Lack of homemade organic matter is, however, an understandable problem for new gardeners, and there sometimes has to be a one-time expense if nothing else is available.

A good deal depends on the time of year the soil is being improved. If the work is being done in the fall, all those leaves that otherwise seem such an intolerable nuisance can come to the rescue. Oak and beech leaves are especially good; maple leaves tend to be soggy. Pile them up—yours and your neighbor's. Run the rotary mower over them (unless you have already rushed out and bought a shredder) and spread them in as thick a layer as you can build up on top of the bare ground. Leaves are excellent organic matter, and they can be rototilled

into the soil together with whatever other extras your test has found your land may need. (Never allow a rototiller to go deeper than one inch into the subsoil whenever it is used; you don't want too much of that inert material incorporated into the growing layer at one time.) If you live by the sea, seaweed straight from the beach without any of the sand or salt washed off can be treated in exactly the same way. Both leaves and seaweed will attract thousands of soil bacteria and worms and will build up the fertility of the land. After the organic matter has been incorporated into the topsoil, pile still more leaves, which can be shredded and put on as they are raked up, over the surface of the soil. If you already have your fence in place the leaves will not blow away. If there is no fence, hold the leaves by spreading chicken wire over them. Black plastic is another possibility, but you must then take measures to hold it down. If you do use plastic, anchor it with rocks and *not* with mounds of dirt, which will grow a bonus of dreadful untidy weeds very early in the spring.

Fall Soil Conditioning
(if you have no or insufficient compost)

Gather leaves.*

Pile them up.

Run rotary mower over them or use shredder.

Spread them over garden plot in thick layer.

Rototill or dig them in.

Shred more leaves and pile them on surface as mulch.

*Or use seaweed straight from the beach.

During the winter this surface leaf layer, which is called a mulch, will slowly decompose and become part of the topsoil. The process will not happen as fast as the decomposition that

is going on with those same leaves underground, but the breakdown will be active enough to leave a greatly shrunken residue that can be easily pushed aside when the time comes to plant. A thick leaf layer will also check the appearance of intrusive spring weeds that go into action long before you are ready to garden. I am against spreading seaweed on top of the ground. Seaweed tends to dry out and separate into rather stringy particles during the winter, through which weeds will grow with ease. Seaweed is also very hard to push aside at planting time; it gets all tangled up with your tools. If you are a neatness demon, or if, like me all those years ago, you have your garden on the front lawn right under the nose of the neighbors, a very tidy method of incorporating organic matter and using it as a mulch is to buy wood chips, sawdust, or the elegant and expensive bark mulch.

Organic material formed from wood is particularly satis-factory for use in **clay soils.** Clay already contains all the water it needs, and the organic matter made from wood does not absorb water and, therefore, will not add to the problem of soil moisture. Wood products also by their structure force clay particles apart when they are mixed together, so in clay soils, organic matter made of decomposing wood serves to speed up water drainage. **Sandy soils** have the opposite problem: water runs through them too fast. The organic matter incorporated into these soils should be absorbent and act like a sponge to keep the water in suspension until the plant roots can make use of it. Shredded or half-decomposed leaves will do the job, and so will any of the peat mosses. With every kind of peat moss it is important to remember that it must be wet before it is mixed into the ground; otherwise it will steal moisture from the surrounding soil rather than holding it in suspension.

With any clay soils it is better to do this type of work in the fall. Even if the ground is wet and big clods form when it is cultivated, these will break down over the winter, so no lasting harm will be done. Digging or rototilling a wet, heavy clay soil in the spring can damage the soil structure. If you cannot get at your land in the fall, and in the spring, lacking other organic matter, decide to use a wood product either in the

ground or on top of it as mulch, there are some extra precautions that have to be taken. Wood, when it first starts to decompose, steals (or borrows is perhaps a better term) nitrogen from the soil. A great deal of nitrogen is needed by soil bacteria to begin the decomposition of wood. In time, as the wood product breaks down still further, this lost nitrogen is returned to the soil. To avoid even a temporary shortage of such an essential element, extra amounts of nitrogen fertilizer should be sprinkled over the ground. There exists a barkwood product marketed under the trade name of Bambe which is already combined with nitrogen fertilizer. This eliminates the nitrogen-stealing problem and is a most excellent product—but it is expensive. Nitrogen fertilizers exist chemically, but there are also plenty of organic nitrogen fertilizers which will do a better job in speeding up the decomposition of wood products because they will not only add nitrogen but also the bacteria that break them down. Dried blood, cottonseed meal, and sludge (Milorganite) are all excellent nitrogen fertilizers with a slight tendency toward acidifying the soil.

Whatever material is used to put organic matter into the soil, it should be added regularly and very lavishly, for the more that is added the richer the topsoil will become and the better its condition. Making sure that the soil contains plenty of some kind of organic material also ensures a proper supply of the various trace elements. These are very rarely needed by plants in more than minute amounts; soil well enriched with organic material will contain those vital minute amounts. The program that I have outlined thus far is fine for the first year of vegetable gardening, and even after that if you have the special problem of a heavy clay or sandy soil, but once the gardening process has been set in motion other forms of organic matter become available and should be collected, allowed to decay so as to become "compost," and then spread on your garden plot.

Compost and how to make it is a subject about which a good deal of hot air has been generated both literally (the process of compost making produces considerable internal heat) and figuratively. It is possible to construct scientific com-

post piles with exactly the right mineral balances that will improve your particular ground by adding various fertilizers, in either chemical or organic forms, and separating the even layers of this enriched plant waste by several inches of plain dirt. We don't go in for that careful manner of compost making. Though I don't doubt that it is effective, it does not suit our life style. We need an enormous amount of compost available at several stages of decomposition, and to produce the quantity of compost needed at speed and in good rich condition, my husband, who has always handled this side of our gardening, has never, after one try, gone in for the enriched or soil-layered method. As organic matter decays, heat builds up, which further assists the breakdown process. It is my husband's contention that turning a compost pile, that is letting air in to fuel the internal fire and getting the outer layer into the heated center (in a manner of speaking, by turning the pile inside out), speeds up the process of decomposition tremendously. A pile carefully layered with soil cannot be turned successfully; the layers get mixed up with one another and the material becomes enormously heavy to move.

Our compost is not very rich; it tests out around 3-2-1, but its structure is first class. It is dark, moist, and crumbly. In its final stage it is not overfine, though any "made" compost left piled up and not incorporated into the soil or laid on top of it will be worked through and through by worms who gradually reduce a slightly coarse structure, which is excellent for plant roots, into an overfine texture. Once a compost pile is ready, it should be used. To leave it piled up is to waste some of its worth. But above all, by my husband's method of compost making we always have enough of it to use it so lavishly that the sheer quantity makes up in part for the low fertility rating.

All sorts of vegetable wastes qualify as materials for making compost. Woody material should not be added unless it is shredded, and even then it must be ground extremely fine. Grass clippings can be added, but most should be used for perpetual mulch (see pages 50–53). Seaweed is an excellent addition to any compost pile, but it must go through a very fine

shredding screen. Seaweed breaks down much more slowly than other organic materials.

Also add to the pile such kitchen debris as carrot, beet, and onion tops, outer leaves of cabbage, grapefruit and orange rinds—anything organic that won't attract dogs and rodents. Strong smelling debris should be buried deeply in the pile. Crush and add as many eggshells as possible, for they add

Compost Ingredients

Yes	No
vegetable tops	woody stalks
outer leaves of lettuce and cabbage	bones and meat scraps
	animal fats
vegetable and fruit table scraps	wood ash (save in watertight container for spring use)
potato peelings	
citrus rinds	used kitty litter
banana skins	certain diseased plant remnants (see page 101)
eggshells	
coffee grounds	
fruit windfalls	
grass clippings	
soft hedge trimmings	
sod	
weeds	
garden remnants	
discarded potted plants	
leaves	
shredded seaweed	
hair clippings	
sawdust	

calcium, which is a very important nutrient. Coffee grounds go in too; these are a source of phosphorus and potash. Windfall apples and other bruised fruits, which are strong in nitrogen and potash, should be included. Banana peels are excellent additions, for they are extremely rich in potash. Bury the kitchen trash as it is added. This is not a big job; you just pull aside a layer of accumulated debris with a hay fork or a clam rake, put in the waste, and cover it up. We do this for aesthetic reasons, for I don't like the look of rotting orange rinds! Don't add used kitty litter to the pile because it is strongly suspected for harboring a virus that will survive composting heat. And no fats, for these bring flies at the best and rats at the worst. Garbage disposals are a luxury which I would be extremely sorry to be without; nevertheless, those who have a compost pile should think hard before they throw good organic waste into the disposal.

Don't add wood ash from winter fires to your pile, for its goodness will be leached away before it is ready to use. We do not deliberately add earth, but a good deal gets into our pile from the soil that adheres to the sod trimmed from stepping stones, from the roots of pulled-out weeds, and from my discarded potted plants.

The process is extremely simple. You need an area in the yard, preferably hidden from public view, with room enough for three bins. These look a little like miniature horse stalls, and, in our case, the dividers that mark them off from each other are old wooden doors. Neater gardeners, or those whose compost making activities have to take place rather more publicly, could build their bins out of lightweight cement building blocks, but the kind of divider does not matter just so long as it exists. There also must be some sort of solid back to each bin. Anything made of wood should be treated with wood preservative. Avoid any material containing creosote, for this has long-lasting toxic properties which pass into the soil.

Each growing season start a new pile early in the spring in whichever bin is empty. Into this put all the winter debris and later all the vegetable wastes of the summer season. In the fall, heap the bin to the bursting point with leaves and with the

cut-down remnants from the garden. We used to chop up all the stalks and stems from tough old plants, but now we throw them on the ground and ride across them with our tractor mower.

Three-Bin / Two-Turn Method of Compost Making

Winter

Last season's organic waste	Empty bin	Season-before-last's organic waste

Spring

1st turning →	Last season's organic waste	Season-before-last's organic waste

Summer

New organic waste	Last season's organic waste	Season-before-last's organic waste

Fall

New organic waste	2nd turning →	Last season's organic waste— half-decomposed (use some of it as winter mulch)

Season-before-last's organic waste as finished compost, ready for use

From then on nature takes its course; you need do absolutely nothing more until the frost leaves the ground in early
spring. This is the season for the first turning, which is done as
soon as the piles thaw out a little. My husband keeps a small
pickax near our pile to loosen it for easy shoveling. Turning
involves throwing the roughly decomposed matter, which will
have shrunk greatly in volume, into the empty bin beside it.
The debris from the outside of the old pile thus moves to the
center of the new pile. Make a little mound in the middle of
the bin and slowly build up around it. In early fall this pile will
be ready for a second shift; this time put into the third bin,
where it will remain until it has decomposed to a topsoil-like
consistency. After turning the pile out of its first bin in the
spring, start a new pile in the emptied area with the waste
organic products of the current season. Composting is a continuous process. Each gardening season there is a bin being
filled with new waste, a second filled with half-decomposed
matter from the first turning, and a third that contains the
almost completed product from the second turning. Depending
on the weather and the length of the frost-free fall season, it
can take from eighteen months to two years for plant wastes
to become completely broken down.

There are all kinds of ways to set about compost making,
which is rapidly evolving from a practical into a countercul-
tural act. I can speak from experience only of the method we
practice. There are also a number of methods for speeding up
the process. Sprinkling a little nitrogen fertilizer on every new
layer of plant matter is an expensive method, but worth it if
you are in a hurry. Some compost makers suggest covering the
pile with a tarpaulin or black plastic to prevent the nutrients
from leaching out. This makes some sense, since anyone who
owns a compost pile knows that lush weeds grow along the
outer edges where the nutrients have seeped away. The trouble
with plastic or any kind of cover is that it has to be taken off
at intervals to moisten the pile, and this I found a great nuisance after trying it for a season. Small quantities of compost
can also be made by those who garden in little containers,
window boxes, or on roof gardens, by stuffing large-size plastic

leaf bags with leaves and layers of soil, moistening this mixture, and then tying the bag tightly and leaving it in a warm place all winter. No odor is caused by this process, and compost should be ready by spring.

In recent years, though we still have our usual piles of compost, I have also been using some garden wastes in a slightly different way. Instead of putting everything on the compost pile, we spread some waste organic matter from the yard thickly over the growing areas to serve as **mulch.** Using a thick mulch has a multitude of advantages; it shades the exposed soil from hot sun and prevents moisture evaporation. Land under a heavy mulch never gets baked, cracked, or dried out. In cold weather it keeps the ground frozen and prevents root heave, particularly important when perennial plants are involved. A sufficiently thick mulch also suppresses weeds which cannot grow without light. Weeds are always a problem, for they too like carefully prepared soil. A mulch to suppress them is, in my opinion, the only answer. I sometimes read criticism of mulching, particularly mulching with hay, because this practice introduces weed seed into the plot. Seed certainly is introduced, but if the mulch is thick and is supplemented regularly throughout the growing season, the weeds will not be able to sprout.

When or if occasional weeds get ahead of you, don't bother to pull them out; just smother them with an extra load of mulch. This is a process that works even with quackgrass and crabgrass, for crabgrass needs full sunlight to grow, so even a little handful of mulch will eliminate it. Growing plants under a heavy mulch does away with the need for summer cultivation with a hoe, which frequently does more harm than good. Vegetables are shallow rooted; so violent, exasperated hoeing often damages the vegetables without making much impact on the weeds! This is a problem that vanishes forever when you garden with a perpetual, constantly renewed mulch.

The **mulching process** should start in the fall after the cleanup of the growing areas. At this stage, gather up all the tattered remnants of the flowers and vegetables and add them to the current compost pile that has been building all summer.

Perpetual Mulching and Fertility Renewing Cycle

Fall/Winter: Spread layer of half-made compost, topped by finished compost, covered by leaves and grass clippings.

Spring: Pull back mulch, spread wood ashes lightly. Plant when ground is ready.

Summer: Pull old mulch back around seedlings. Add new mulch to make a thick layer impervious to sun but not to water. Keep mulch renewed and cover all spots bared by harvesting.

Next spread half-decomposed compost from the middle pile over the growing plot, about 2 inches deep. This material is still very coarse and rough and not the least like topsoil, but all the soil organisms are fiercely active in it, and during the winter the final stages of decomposition will take place. If the soil tests show the area needs lime, which happens about every third year, this is the time to put it on—on top of the half-decayed compost. Over the lime goes a second layer of finished compost laid down thickly enough to cover completely the half-decomposed material. Spreading finished compost on top of half-decayed organic matter speeds up the decomposition process. Finally we pile on the leaves and grass clippings that are picked up by the grass catcher during the long, lovely days of Indian summer, when grass obstinately continues to grow no matter how much you yearn to put away the lawn mower. Dump this loose mixture on the plot in untidy heaps and spread it around with a bamboo rake. I try to have the ground go into winter with several inches of this leaf and grass mixture on it. In rare years when cold weather comes early and the grass stops grow-

ing before the final mulch goes on, just use leaves by themselves. We do have to be careful of one thing when using grass in the fall. Our lawns are bordered with pine trees, which throw down a carpet of discarded needles in early fall. Pine needles are intensely acid, too much so for good vegetable growth, and I try to keep them out of the grass and leaf mulch. This is all you need to do, and all we've done for years, and my soil tests show no need for extra fertilizer in the fall, though I do sometimes add some during the growing season.

In the spring, as soon as frost begins to leave the ground and the early vegetable seeds should be planted, clear mulch from a section of ground sufficiently large for them and prevent the mulch from blowing back by standing two boards on edge and roughly pegging them into position with stakes. At this point, spread wood ashes lightly over the newly exposed soil, and work them in. Wood ashes are an excellent source of calcium, potassium, and lesser amounts of various trace elements, but since they also contain lime, do not lay them on too thickly. The soil, having been kept cold by the mulch, takes one or two weeks, depending on the weather, to warm up and become ready for planting. Nevertheless, the moment the mulch is pulled back the appearance of the earth underneath is a delight. It is dark, beautifully textured, and full of decayed organic material. As it warms up it also becomes full of worms with their highly fertile castings. You can be certain if soil was kept under mulch all winter that it will never be too dry or too fine. When the first rows of seed are tall enough to be clear of the danger of smothering, pull up the boards and lay the mulch back by hand between the rows. This will obliterate weeds that have also germinated. Everything that grows from seed or is set out as preraised plants is handled the same way.

As soon as the grass needs to be cut, the clippings are spread between the rows of growing plants over the remains of the winter leaf mulch, and any areas that are not yet planted are always kept heavily mulched. Little plants and rows of seedlings should have the mulch drawn as close to them as possible. Grass heats up fast if it is left as a big pile. It then becomes airless, heavy, slimy, and very smelly; in this state it

also attracts flies that breed in it. Grass clippings should, therefore, always be added to a compost pile well mixed in with
other organic waste products. But grass clippings spread an
inch or so deep each time as mulch, and allowed to dry out
slightly before another layer is added, smell only faintly of cut
hay and produce no problems. We happen to have a great deal
of grass and huge quantities of clippings. For years I was afraid
to use them, as I had read so much about their capacity to
generate intense heat. But I have no problem of this sort and
find it's a wonderful way to have constant, free mulching
material always available. Do not use grass clippings, however,
if a herbicide weedkiller has been used on the lawn.

But maybe you've turned your lawn into the vegetable plot
and have no grass clippings. What happens then? Half-decomposed compost, though heavier to drag around, makes an excellent mulch as long as it is still in a rough enough stage that

Peppers

weeds will not grow in it. Garden wastes put through a shredder are good too, and in this case you can have the shredder beside the vegetable plot, thus saving yourself a lot of work. Newspaper can also do a fine job. Lay five or six sheets of paper down between the rows or over any open space. Since paper is wood pulp, sprinkle a nitrogen fertilizer over it. If you don't like the look of a paper mulch, and few of us do, it can be covered with whatever grass you can find or wood chips or any of the peat mosses which are readily available in bales at garden stores. Most people hearing the word "mulch" think only of peat moss, and they think of it only in terms of neatness, for it tidies up a plot. Peat moss has many admirable qualities, but it does not make a good mulch when used alone. It dries out very easily and then becomes impermeable to water. Rain cannot penetrate a very thick layer of dried-out peat moss. It also shrinks as it dries and exposes bare soil, and weeds leap into these open breaches. Peat moss can, however, be safely used to cover newspaper and keep the garden looking nicer. A drawback of a very thick newspaper mulch is that in a dry season it may not decompose quickly enough to be pulled apart for later plantings.

Whatever you use for year-round mulch, the method will change your gardening life. I've used this system on my vegetable plot for the last fifteen years, and during that time the soil has never once been turned over. There has been no digging or rototilling, for none is needed. As soon as the leaves are pulled back wonderful soil is ready for me, without any waiting around for a man with a plow. I read that perpetual mulching brings on fearful invasions of snails and slugs; I can only say that such plagues have never troubled me. I have slugs (who doesn't?), but I find their trails more on the path between the vegetable plots than among the vegetables themselves. Also, rather oddly, I've had no trouble with cutworms since I took up this style of vegetable gardening, and I used to be plagued with them when we rototilled.

It could be difficult for owners of very large vegetable plots to garden this way, for it might be hard to get enough mulch all summer long to keep the level high. But gardeners with

large plots would be well advised to use mulch around plants that suffer badly in dry weather—tomatoes and cucumbers for example—perhaps leaving a few unmulched plants as an experiment. I am prepared to wager a small bet that the mulched plants will carry a heavier, healthier crop. Half my gardening life in this country was spent growing vegetables the conventional way with annual digging, regular incorporation of organic matter into the soil, and laborious weeding. The other half has been spent gardening under mulch. I could no longer grow vegetables in the quantities I do were I to return to the conventional method.

I am not much in favor of black plastic as a mulch. I've tried it, and I thought it damaged the soil structure by preventing rain from passing through. I have, however, found it excellent laid down in small areas with slits cut in it for melons. These seem to ripen faster and grow bigger and juicier when they spread over the warm plastic. There are numerous possible mulch materials in various parts of the country. Spent hop vines are excellent; chopped sugar cane is very good; salt hay makes a wonderful mulch. The only necessity, whatever you use, is that the mulch should be spread so thickly that it blocks light from the soil but permits the entrance of water, and that it is kept renewed during the growing season. Being organic, it too will be attacked by soil bacteria and will shrink astonishingly fast. By fall an 8-inch-thick spring layer in the vegetable plot will have thinned down into a pitiable little remnant that will need to be renewed with the perpetual fertile cycle of a layer of half-made compost, topped by finished compost, that is covered in turn by leaves and grass.

Tools
and
Supplies

 Where special equipment for vegetable growing is involved, move slowly and, like Uriah Heep, start *umbly*. Unless in the past you have given the care of your yard completely to a gardening service and don't have a single gardening tool on the place, the chances are excellent that the tools used to keep the grass and flowers in order will be quite sufficient for vegetable growing with a few rather minor purchases. There are some additional, slightly lavish, pieces of equipment that may in time seem worth buying, but not at first. It is far better to use what's around and keep the purse strings closed until you are certain, through practical experience, what is really needed.

Every outdoor gardener ought to own either a straight-sided short-handled **spade,** a short-handled, wide-tined **garden fork,** or a long-handled **shovel.** You don't necessarily need all three; it's a matter of which type of tool you, and your back, find the easiest to use for a prolonged stretch of work. This is the tool needed to turn over the soil (something some gardeners still like to do each year), dig up plants like rhubarb and large perennials that should be divided, and dig potatoes if they are raised in the traditional manner. I don't think it is possible to do any kind of gardening without either a spade or a shovel, so this should be No. 1 on any list. Make sure if you are buying this tool for the first time that you get one that feels

well balanced when you handle it: the working head should not feel enormously heavy, and the handle should suit your hand.

Tools come in many weights and sizes, and they need the same slow careful choice as a tennis racket.

If the store stocks only one size, try somewhere else and go on searching until you find something that seems right for you personally. I would suggest avoiding, even in these inflationary times, cut-rate, inexpensive tools; go for the middle range if you must economize. But with most tools, the most expensive is usually by far the best.

A good **rake** with iron tines or teeth is an extremely important tool. Rakes are used to break up lumps in the soil and to gather in the stones that rise to the surface during the winter months. A rake is used, therefore, to get the soil into a fine pulverized condition so that seed can be sown in it. Rakes come in many sizes, some with wide heads and long teeth and others with tiny stubby little teeth. We seem to have them in all sizes, but I use only one, a medium-small rake with a head 10 inches across and teeth 2 inches long. I find larger rakes rather tiring to use, though that might not trouble a younger gardener. They also leave the soil too rough for seeding, and everything has to be gone over again with a short-tined rake. I always skip two-stage work if there is a possible alternative, and the medium-size rake I use works very well for my style of gardening. You will also need a bamboo lawn rake for gathering up debris.

A **hoe** is another necessity. A hoe is used for weeding primarily by tearing plant intruders, roots and all, out of the soil when the sharp blade, at right angles to the handle, is pulled toward the gardener. Most hoeing of weeds is done with a straight-ended hoe, but there are also pointed hoes and a flat hoe that has an edge on both sides and will decapitate weeds when it is pushed forward or dragged back—this is known as the Dutch or scuffle hoe. For the unmulched vegetable garden, the scuffle hoe is recommended; it will do the least harm to plants. I no longer use a hoe to get out weeds; I take a different course, which is to smother them with mulch, some

form of deep covering in which weed seed will not germinate. This takes away the traditional need for a hoe. So why am I suggesting you need one? A hoe is still an important tool, because it is ideal to open a furrow for sowing seed. I use the traditional flat-bladed garden hoe with the blade at right angles to the handle to make these furrows, and I use the edge of it for the job. I much prefer this type of hoe for making vital furrows than a pointed hoe.

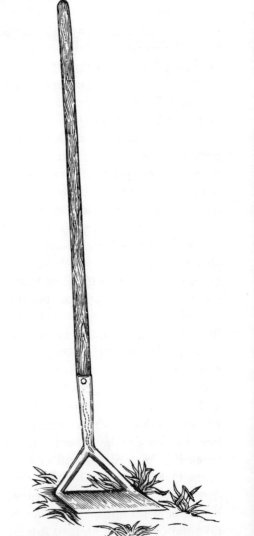

Dutch scuffle hoe

A **trowel** is another necessity. It has many uses, but the most important is to make planting holes for hot-weather crops that have to be set out individually, or for thinnings that have to be lifted and replanted in one quick operation. An iron trowel with a wooden handle is by far the best buy, though mysteriously these are getting extremely hard to find. Beware of trowels with thin metal blades that bend; they make any job twice as hard. Beware also of a trowel that is all metal, the handle included. These raise appalling blisters. Another essential is a waterproof kneeling pad. There's no need to buy special individual tie-ons for each knee; those are nothing but a gimmick. Get a seat pad from an auto accessory shop and mark one side with a splash of red paint to prevent kneeling on the wet side when you move the pad to the next position!

A **hose** is also necessary, as well as something to hang it on. Many gadgets are sold as hose supports, but we hang ours on lengths of redwood nailed to trees or fence posts. But whatever arrangements you make, have something near the faucet on which the hose can be coiled up off the ground. A hose left lying around looks particularly untidy; it is a hazard when you walk around in the evening; it will kill the grass underneath it on a single hot day; and it will get badly damaged by mowers and wheelbarrows going over it. Furthermore, a hose left lying around undrained in hot weather will heat up almost to boiling point, and the first gush of water can scald plants fatally. By the same count, a hose left lying on the ground with water still in it in the fall can freeze and rupture the casing.

All kinds of tricky attachments are sold to use with a hose, few of which are really essential. I would leave them as nice presents for the family to give you on special occasions! An exception: if you are linking several hose sections, "quick connectors" which snap together are a great help. There are also plastic connectors with simple cut-off switches which allow you to turn water on and off without returning to the faucet; these are invaluable for preventing drenchings when sprinklers must be moved. Many gardeners use **sprinklers** to irrigate their crops: if you prefer this method, one of the best is the type that swings to and fro, covering a lot of ground in the

process. All sprinklers should be adjustable—otherwise they waste water—and most of them need the apertures kept regularly cleaned out with a pin or a straightened paper clip if they are to work properly.

Suggested Basic Equipment for Vegetable Growing

Spade, shovel, or garden fork according to personal preference
Medium-small garden rake
Bamboo rake
Scuffle hoe
Trowel
Kneeling pad
Hose
Plastic watering cans
Hay fork

Wheelbarrow or cart
Soil-testing kit
Cold frame
Small-plant protectors
Pipe and wire for plant-supporting trellis
Chicken wire, netting or twine for plant supports
Sturdy stakes
Sharpening tool

A drawback to watering by sprinkling is the way in which it wets the foliage of plants rather than directing the moisture straight to the roots. Plants enjoy some moisture on their leaves but not so much that the ground below them remains dust-dry. Plants also should never be allowed to go into a hot humid night with wet foliage, for this sets up pestilential mildew. To avoid that problem, and still have the hose cover a lot of ground when it is in use, **canvas soil soakers** are available through which water slowly seeps the entire length, and also **perforated hoses** with dozens of tiny pinholes through which water escapes. Both of these are admirable ideas, but they are difficult to use. Laying a length of dirty and often wet canvas hose in and out and roundabout the rows of vegetables is a muddy, exasperating job. The canvas makes sharp kinks at

every turn, which cuts the flow of the water, and it is hard to lay it down without injuring the foliage of plants at the ends of the row. Getting it out is even worse. It can't be yanked out because of the loops and turns around the plantings. Yet walking over the wet ground lifting the messy thing out compacts the earth and drives out vital air. The perforated hose is, if possible, even more exasperating to handle. All perforations are supposed to lie against the soil and penetrate it deeply. But being much more rigid than the canvas soaker, the hose will arch as the water runs through, and many of the perforations turn upward and send a thin stream of wasteful water either beyond the growing area or at least where it is not wanted. Getting it out is just as troublesome as the soaker, and more hazardous, since a hose retains water and invariably squirts it over you as you struggle to unwind it from the garden. With either of these delights, you will end up hot, cross, wet, and dirty. For this reason, and because we often run short of water in our area in dry summers, I prefer to use a **water wand** made of aluminum that has a round diffuser on the far end that breaks the force of the water as it gushes out and diminishes the likelihood of soil washout. These are sold as "bubblers," they fasten onto the hose, can be poked safely among rows of vegetables without hurting them, and will get the water exactly where you need it without any waste and without wetting the foliage. They are well worth their price.

If you don't have one and are getting washout when you run the hose, put a shingle under the hose outflow to break and distribute the force of the water. If you have no shingle you can use the blade of your spade laid flat on the ground with the hose end draped over it. Vegetable gardeners also need **watering cans;** don't let anyone tell you that they are obsolete. In these times of increasing water shortages they are invaluable. There should be at least two, one as large as you can handle and a small one for fiddling little jobs. Both should be of plastic to cut the weight, and the most useful are those with a long spout and a wide neck for easy filling. A rose, the diffuser that breaks up the water as it comes through the spout, is not necessary, though most good cans are sold with one.

Three or four large **plastic garbage cans** complete with lids

are great time savers. Used as trash cans and set at the four corners of the plot, they save a lot of untidiness as well as many journeys to the compost pile. You can collect weeds and every sort of organic trash in them, and empty this out only as the cans fill up. Big trash cans can also double as water storage units in times of drought.

A **wheelbarrow** or some sort of **cart** to move soil and mulch and take the rubbish to the compost is also essential, and here I am going to suggest an extravagance. Pass up all those conventional little carts and single-wheeled barrows that are on sale at hardware stores and garden centers, and send away for a well-balanced cart high off the ground on big pneumatic wheels. Two firms in Vermont (Vermont-Ware, Hinesburg 05461, and Garden-Way Research, Charlotte 05445) will ship these carts in several sizes anywhere. There are probably many other distributors as well. We came late to these carts; my husband had always used the traditional wooden wheelbarrow with removable sides, and I had used a small metal version with low sides. I gave my husband one of the special

Large-wheeled garden cart

carts for Christmas twenty years ago after he had been ill. From that day on, he has never touched the old wheelbarrow. The carts do big jobs in half the time with much less effort than is needed with a conventional barrow, and they are worth every penny of their not inconsiderable cost.

Another necessity in my eyes is some kind of **soil-testing kit.** This is a one-time expense that can make all the difference to the success of your garden; far too few people bother to use them. (See pages 33–35).

Brand-new vegetable gardeners usually start off buying their hot-weather plants: the tomatoes, cucumbers, melons, squash, peppers, and eggplants. But this phase soon ends as it becomes obvious that money can be saved and much better varieties produced by raising these plants at home. This method, which is not hard, is outlined on pages 135 ff. But what is more tricky is getting house-raised plants acclimatized and able to be set outdoors in the ground. There is an intermediate stage known as "hardening off" that simply cannot be skipped. This is best accomplished by means of a **cold frame,** which is essentially a bottomless box set on the ground facing south with, if possible, the back a little higher than the front and some form of removable cover, either of glass or one of the new rigid clear plastics. Cold frames, as described on pages 143–45, can be cheap or costly, but provision must be made for having something of that sort if home horticulture of hot-weather plants is to be a success. This is a one-time expense that rapidly amortizes itself, since gardeners find a dozen extra uses for a cold frame once they have it.

Once the little plants are over that stage and in the ground they often need protection in fickle spring weather against sudden cold or tearing wind, either of which can stunt their growth irreparably. Many **protective devices** are sold by gardening stores to put over the plants, but they are an unnecessary expense. Some such protective item is essential, but don't spend money buying anything. Cut the bottoms and tops out of waxed or plastic milk cartons, bleach or detergent bottles, or other large containers, accumulate several dozen of these during the winter, and you will have the recycled means of

protecting newly set-out tender plants. Sunk deeply into the ground around a small plant, recycled milk cartons also protect against that devastating springtime night prowler the cutworm. If you live in a rural area, look around to see how other gardeners protect their plants. In the North, discarded bottomless sap buckets are widely used for large plants. Your area may feature some other usable discard.

Many gardeners like to take a chance on rows of vegetables, bush beans in particular, a little ahead of the date when they really should be planted. Other gardeners like to get a head start on everything once the ground is workable even if the air is still cold. Impatient gardeners of this sort should lay in a store of croquet-wicket-like wire hoops made from the long side of wire coat hangers and a couple of rolls of thick but pliable transparent plastic with which they can cover and anchor down protection for emerging crops. The equipment for this early-bird gardening should be laid in well ahead of time.

Vegetable gardeners invariably also need something to train or tie tall plants up against. A lightweight **trellis** is an excellent support for peas, climbing beans, tomatoes, and cucumbers. This can be easily set up in different parts of the growing area year after year using galvanized pipe 1 inch in diameter in 5- or 6-foot lengths. The pipes, which can be bought and cut to order at building and plumbing supply outlets, should be driven with a heavy mallet into the ground a foot deep and about 5 feet apart. (You can get them out very easily when the season is over by rocking them to and fro.) Once in, they should be linked with strong wire tied tightly around the end poles and looped several times around those in between. Try to keep this wire as taut as possible, and run three strands of it from pole to pole, one at the top, one in the center, and one at ground level. This makes the framework of the trellis. The uprights against which the plants grow can be tall stakes tied to the wires (which I find too rigid a method), netting, twine, or chicken wire. I prefer to use lengths of chicken wire wrapped around the end poles and tied with thin wire to the wire framework. Except in the tremendously hot areas of the country there is no need to buy expensive plastic-

covered wire to insulate the plant against heat from the sun. Chicken wire can become hot, but this is a problem I have rarely run into. I use chicken wire as the background support for tall tomatoes, cucumbers, and peas. When the vine growth becomes very heavy I give additional support by running lengths of cord from pole to pole across the front of the vines and thus holding them closer and more firmly to the trellis. With beans, twine looped to and fro from top to bottom wire will serve as the climbing support. Beans grow by twisting around something, not by tendrils like cucumbers or needing support like tomatoes.

Every such trellis is highly wind resistant even before the plants start to grow up it and will also throw considerable shade. That is why trellises should always be planned for the back of the lot and never expected to withstand strong wind unless the supporting pipes are a foot in the ground. This kind of trellis does not take long to put up, and it should go in very early in spring as soon as you can work outdoors before the great planting rush starts. The specific parts may cost a little the first time, but apart from the twine, they are all reusable and take up very little storage space.

Chicken-wire trellis for peas, climbing beans, tomatoes, and cucumbers

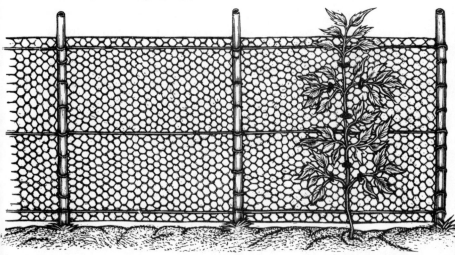

Pole beans will also climb up reasonably thin rough **poles** if you can find any. A polished smooth stake will not do unless you wind string around it so that the twisting vine can get a purchase. Bean poles can be planted in tepee fashion, slanted with the three poles that form the base fairly far apart and the tops tied together. The seed is then planted beside each pole. Strong wooden posts can also be driven into the ground and wire strung from them exactly as is done with the iron pipes as a support for twine. I have given up using long wooden posts; I found them hard to get into the ground and hold steady, and they were far less manageable when I wanted to change the growing area.

Main-crop tomatoes can also be grown confined in a circular **wire-cage.** The best wire for this is "sheep wire," a 6-inch square mesh or the kind of mesh that is used in cement construction. This will be hard to handle and may prove to be a two-man job. It is the most useful for caged tomatoes because the wide mesh enables you to get your hand in and the fruit out. I make my cages 2-2½ feet in diameter, and where the wire overlaps I cut and bend the ends to make hooks that hold the cage together. To hold it steady I again use iron pipe threaded through the mesh and driven very deeply into the ground. Tomato stems do best tied to the cage. I have never found twisting a tomato stem around a support to work— though I constantly see it advised. Wire that has been coiled to make a cage has to be straightened out for winter storage, unless you have plenty of room and can store the cages as are. If you mean to pile them up somewhere outdoors, be careful where you put them. I once laid mine down in a place where, unknown to me, poison ivy existed. By the time I came to get the cages in the spring the worst had happened, and I had to get help from a friend who, happily, is immune to this nuisance!

Every garden needs plenty of **stakes,** which can be bought for quite a cost at garden centers. These are useful for early tomatoes, eggplant, peppers, and innumerable small jobs. Get strong stakes despite the cost; avoid thin bamboo stakes, for they are too fragile for vegetables. Stakes should have the

business end dipped in old crankcase oil or a wood preservative to save them from rot. If they break, resharpen the ends; this halves the effort of driving them into the ground. All stakes should be pulled out when the plot is cleaned up in the fall, and they should be stored under cover in the winter. A very useful adjunct to a vegetable plot are the brass rods that once carried curtains or held down stair carpet; if you come upon these, treasure them. They are invaluable for threading through chicken wire to hold temporary fencing, winter or summer, to keep out rabbits and dogs, or to keep the leaf mulch tidily enclosed.

If you already own a **riding mower,** a cart that can be hitched up behind it is a great time saver. Don't buy a **tractor** with all its manifold attachments unless you mean to go in for vegetable gardening on an almost homesteading scale and unless you have ample storage space. Tractors are expensive workhorses unsuited to small-scale vegetable growing except as a status symbol. I feel rather the same about the "in" piece of equipment, the **shredder.** Shredders grind organic matter in varying sizes according to the mesh of the screen you use; most shredders come with varying size screens. Shredding organic matter, the debris from the garden and leaves, does speed up the process of compost making and provides excellent mulch, that inert covering on which weeds won't grow. What's more, a shredder can be taken to the vegetable plot to do the mulching on the spot, which is a time saver. But shredders are expensive: they already cost over $100 and will inevitably go up. They are noisy to operate and use gasoline. They also can be extremely tiring, in spite of the alluring advertisements, for those screens clog easily. I owned an early hand-operated shredder. It worked on the principle of a meat grinder with a huge crank handle. It did a good job when we felt strong enough to get it out and use it. But more and more it lay unused in the back of the shed, and we cut up the rough, coarse material for the compost pile by hand. Now that I am not strong enough to crank the old shredder, I have felt no need to buy a mechanical one. Yet many excellent gardeners swear by them and say they cut the labor in half, so this must be a

matter of your personal choice. If you own a rotary mower there is no need to buy a shredder to pulverize dry leaves and all but the largest garden waste. Pile it up and run the mower over and through the pile several times. Treating the leaves and other organic waste in this way will go even faster if the chute of the mower is angled toward a wall or solid fence so that the cut-up material will ricochet back under the blade of the mower and thus get ground up into even smaller pieces.

For handling a compost pile a **hay fork** and a **clam rake** are invaluable. We use them for lifting and turning the half-made material and for letting air into the pile. We also use the hay fork for spreading half-made compost on the soil. A light-weight small **pickax** is also useful for loosening up compost that has settled down into a solid mass during the winter.

Rototillers are another extravagance. These are expensive machines that need good mechanical attention to stay in proper working order. They also take up a great deal of storage room. Most of them are bone-shaking horrors to use; the vibrations they set up have nothing in common with good vibes! Tillers do exist that have the engine in front of the revolving prongs; these are less hard to run and to steer, as I discovered when I tested one owned by a friend. But to my mind this is a dubious purchase, since rototillers are rentable, sometimes with a man to operate them. Just look under "rental equipment" in the yellow pages or inquire at a garden center. I don't happen to manage my garden in a manner that calls for rototilling; if I did I would always hire and never buy.

I don't go in for winter oiling against rust, though I often see it advised. I keep our tools clean and I use them too much for rust to accumulate. I do hang them up on a pegboard.

Sharpening is more important than most people realize; a sharp shovel or hoe is a snap to use.

To sharpen our tools we use a small **electric grinder;** hand-cranked models are also available. This is perhaps a mild luxury; a file will sharpen tools as well, though not nearly as quickly.

I have no **sprayers** and no **spray tanks** because I have no

regular spray program. For advice about these you must look elsewhere, but regarding sprays, dusts, and other deterrents to plant diseases see pages 150–61. Most of my tools have been in use for over thirty years—those rakes belonging to my predecessor for more than half a century. So even if hand tools cost more than you expect, they will last you forever. Tools can become a compulsion and a horrid expense; thousands of gadgets do not a gardener make. And haste makes dreadful waste where garden tools are concerned. Take your time about innovations; look at someone else's purchase before you buy something for yourself. If I had ever seen a soil soaker in action in someone else's yard, I would never have bought that monstrous object, so let my experience serve as a caution to all new gardeners.

Getting Ready

Long before the first magic moment of planting arrives, both new and experienced gardeners need to plan what plants they mean to grow in order to send for the necessary **seeds.** As a result of the present boom in home gardening some of the better varieties of vegetable seeds are beginning to be in short supply, and forethought on many counts is highly important. Satisfactory crops can be grown from seeds bought from racks at garden centers, hardware stores, or even from the supermarket and the five and ten. These seeds are all marketed by reputable seedsmen and, so long as the proper date is stamped on them, are both fresh and good. Indeed, in a sudden crisis I'm apt to pick up a spare package this way myself.

The vital difference between rack seeds and those bought from catalogs appears when your particular growing area has less than perfect conditions. Or you may need special kinds of seeds to suit your particular problem: early-maturing varieties, for example, for an area subject to very early frosts. Rack seeds are perfectly adequate for optimum conditions, but they're not marketed to fit special needs. By contrast, when you order seed from a catalog it's possible to choose among a great quantity of varieties for every vegetable and find the type that not only suits your culinary tastes or your plot's individual growing requirements, but also has bred into it new and powerful pro-

tectors from some of the diseases that now haunt vegetables. Seed catalogs also sell you the new hybrids long before these appear on the open racks.

Many seed catalogs still come free for the asking. A single postcard to one seed house often produces a deluge of other catalogs, for your name may then go onto many lists. Other firms charge a small sum for their catalogs. The list here shows the firms that I and other vegetable growers have found the most useful. A call to the state extension service, the local county agent, or your local horticultural society, or a visit to a garden center in your area, will usually provide the names and addresses of still other seedsmen who may specialize in seeds for your particular part of the country.

It is sometimes difficult for a new gardener to estimate how much seed to buy.

For the most part the smallest size seed package is quite enough,

and it is important to guard against feeling that every seed in every package *must* be used not only in order to have enough crops but in order not to waste the seed. Most books are inclined to suggest that seed cannot be carried over from year to year, but this has certainly not proved to be true in my case. After I've opened a package and sown as much of its contents as I need at that moment, I reseal the package. If the package is foil, do not close it up too tightly. I then put the half-used packages into a jar (I happen to use large freeze-dried coffee jars), screw back the lid, and store the jar on the shelf at the back of the refrigerator for the remainder of the summer. This seed remains perfectly usable later on in the season and usually is viable, that is, still full of life, the next year as well. In the winter I store leftover seed in an unheated shed. If you have any doubts about its viability, you can test it out by scattering a few seeds on a washcloth and place it in a warm, dark place. If no signs of sprouting appear at all after a couple of weeks, then throw out the remainder of the package and buy fresh seeds. Normally there will be enough germination, even though it may be a little less than the previous year, to be

Seed Sources

Agway, Box 1333, Syracuse, N.Y. 13201.

Archias Seed Store, 106 E. Main St., Sedalia, Mo. 65301.

Burgess Seed & Plant Co., Galesburg, Mich. 49053.

Burnett Brothers, 92 Chambers St., New York, N.Y. 10007.

W. Atlee Burpee Co., 300 Park Ave., Warminster, Penna. 18974; Clinton, Iowa 52732; Riverside, Calif. 92504.

D. V. Burrell Seed Growers Co., Rocky Ford, Colo. 81067.

Carter's Tested Seeds Ltd., Raynes Park, London S.W. 20, England.

Correvon Fils et Cie, 1225 Cheve-Bourg, Geneva, Switzerland.

De Giorgi Co., 1411 3rd St., Council Bluffs, Iowa 51501.

Samuel Dobie & Son Ltd., 11 Grosvenor Square, Chester, England.

Farmer Seed & Nursery Co., Faribault, Minn. 55021.

Henry Field Seed Co., Shenandoah, Iowa 51601.

Glecklers Seedmen, Metamora, Ohio 43540.

Greene Herb Garden, Greene, R.I. 02827.

Gurney Seed Co., Yankton, South Dakota 57078.

Joseph Harris Co., Moreton Farm, Rochester, N.Y. 14624.

J. L. Hudson, Seedsman, Box 1058, Redwood City, Calif. 94064.

Johnny Apple Seeds, Acton, Mass. 01720.

J. W. Jung Seed Co., Randolph, Wisc. 53956.

Kitazawa Seed Co., 356 W. Taylor St., San Jose, Calif. 95110.

D. Landreth Seed Co., 2700 Wilmarco Ave., Baltimore, Md. 21223.

Le Jardin du Gourmet, Ramsey, N.J. 07446 (a good source for shallots and leek plants).

Earl May Seed & Nursery Co., Shenandoah, Iowa 51603.

Natural Development Co., Box 215, Bainbridge, Penna. 17502.

Nichols Garden Nursery, 1190 North Pacific Highway, Albany, Ore. 97321.

L. L. Olds Seed Co., Box 1069, Madison, Wisconsin 53701.

Geo. W. Park Seed Co., Greenwood, S.C. 29647.

Seedway, Inc., Hall, N.Y. 14463.

R. H. Shumway, Seedsman, Rockford, Ill. 61101.

Stokes Seeds, Box 548, Buffalo, N.Y. 14240.

Sutton Seeds Ltd., Reading, Berks, England.

Thomas Seeds, Winthrop, Maine 04364.

Thompson & Morgan Ltd., London Rd., Ipswich 1P2oBA,
   Suffolk, England, and Box 24, Somerdale, N.J. 08083.
Otis S. Twilley Seed Co., Salisbury, Md. 21801.
W. J. Unwin Ltd., Histon, Cambridge, England.
Vesey's Seeds, York, Prince Edward Island, Canada (good for
   short-season seeds).
Vilmorin-Andrieux, Service Exportation, Boite Postal 30-01,
   75-Paris-R.P., France.

perfectly adequate for the whole vegetable crop. Seed does
deteriorate if it is allowed to get damp, or if it's kept in too hot
a place. But cold does not apparently affect even the seed of
tender plants such as eggplant or tomato.

Seed tape is also available now from many seed houses.
This is a water-soluble tape into which tiny seed is embedded.
In theory this is an excellent way for the new gardener to
eliminate some of the problems of planting. In practice these
tapes do not work out all that well—at least in my own experience. I have found it hard to get the tape to lie evenly on the
seed bed, so the germination was, in consequence, spotty. The
careful spacing of the seed, though it proved a very good indication of what I ought to do when I sow seed by hand, left
much less margin for the disasters that come from weather,
disease, or even the cat's getting into the vegetable plot—
problems that most of us remedy by using the extras we've
accumulated by sowing rather too thickly in the first place.
Also, there are not nearly as many varieties of specific vegetables available in seed tape as exist as plain package seed; the
choice is much more limited. Nevertheless, the fact that I did
not have much luck with seed tapes after a couple of years of
experimentation should certainly not be taken as a final and
definitive reason for not trying them yourself. Gardening is
never boring, just because there is always something new
around the corner waiting to be tested even in the most amateurish way, and for those who've never used seed tape I would
suggest trying it out at least once. But realize that this way of

growing vegetables is much more expensive; seed tape costs a great deal more than package seed. Pelleted seeds, specially coated to make them larger and more manageable, are also available in rather limited varieties. They too are more expensive.

Before you order what is becoming an increasingly expensive product, consider very dispassionately the tastes of those you intend to feed. If you're a family that eats a tremendous amount of salad or has a soup and sandwich lunch daily throughout the summer, lettuce, tomatoes, spinach or its hot-weather equivalent, and onions should loom large in the planting plan. If everyone worries about his weight and doesn't touch potatoes, that solves another problem—if your garden is large enough to grow potatoes in the first place. If, because potatoes are never eaten, two vegetables are consumed at every meal, most novice and amateur gardeners with small plots have to settle for growing at home only those vegetables that taste much better freshly harvested and continue to rely, in part, on store-bought vegetables to fill in the gaps. Don't try out too many unknowns in a single season; one new taste experience every year is usually quite enough for most families, particularly if there are children around. If you want to go in strongly for herbs, remember that these need not take up precious room in the vegetable plot. They can be grown in other places in the yard.

If you're anxious to grow **surplus crops to freeze, can, pickle, or store,** look for the varieties marked in the seed catalogs as being particularly suited to this. And, if you haven't already done so, you must also give some thought to the equipment and materials you'll need. Just as seeds are in short supply in the late spring, canning jars and lids disappear from the market shelf precisely when you most need them. Advance planning is essential.

Frozen vegetables are probably the easiest to process, as they require only a short blanching period, rapid cooling, and packaging. You can also freeze vegetables by cooking them in the same way you would for the table, except shorten the cooking time by about five minutes, and hermetically seal them in boilable cooking pouches. Electric sealing devices for

these bags are marketed under such names as Seal-a-Meal and Meals in Minutes. If you don't already own a freezer or if you count pennies on your electric bill, canning is probably the most economical way to process surplus vegetables. Vegetables high in acid content (tomatoes and rhubarb), pickles, fruits, jams, and preserves can be processed in a simple boiling-water bath, but other vegetables require processing in a steam-pressure canner. For an excellent, simple guide to freezing and canning techniques see the *Blue Book* published by the Ball Corporation, manufacturers of glass jars.

If you have a cool (but above freezing) dry basement or other storage area, you may want to consider storing some vegetables there and adjusting your seed requirements and planting plans accordingly. Onions can be dried in the sun for a few days and then hung in mesh bags in a dry, well-ventilated place such as an attic or unheated room. Winter squashes and pumpkins, with a piece of stem left on them when harvested, can be "cured" for ten days or so at 80–85 degrees and then stored in a dry place at 55–60 degrees. Root crops such as beets, carrots, and turnips keep best between 32 and 40 degrees. To preserve their crispness they need to be embedded in layers of moist sand, peat, or sphagnum moss. They can also be stored in plastic bags that have had ventilation holes cut in them. But whatever method you choose for processing or storing surplus vegetables, you will be well advised to make advance preparations. At the very least you should consider all the alternatives and plan the size and content of your garden plot with your storage resources in mind.

During the first year of vegetable growing, no matter how many charts you draw, or what kind of flags, daggers, and asterisks you put on them for varying situations, there's really no way to be sure how much you should plant, except through trial and error. If you find you've underplanted and do not have enough of what you want, that at least is a yardstick for another year. If you overplant and haven't the time to can or freeze the surplus, you can gain consolation either by handing out largess to your less fortunate neighbors or by building up a magnificent compost pile of surplus organic matter for your

garden next year! All this is excusable the first time around, but it should not happen the second year.

> Every vegetable gardener should keep some kind of record of what varieties he grows and how they do. The notes should also include the dates of the first plantings, the last spring frost, and the first fall frost. It should contain a rough drawing of the planting plan, to eliminate the hazard of putting the same crop in the same place in consecutive years. The weather should also be noted: whether it's dry or wet, or cold or even abnormally windy.

All this information is of great importance in the second year of vegetable gardening, because it can help you estimate fairly closely how much of every crop your family will eat and you can handle.

But what about the first year? What on earth is the new gardener to do? In "Site and Size" the amount of vegetables that can be grown successfully in plots of different sizes was discussed. With this information in mind, with the knowledge of your family tastes, and with a scale drawing of your plot in front of you, **lay out on paper which vegetable you intend to grow where.** Vegetables fall into two categories: those that stay in the plot all summer long and are planted only once (tomatoes, for example) and those that come quickly to maturity and then are either replanted or replaced with a different fast-maturing crop (lettuce and radishes for example). Two root vegetables, carrots and beets, and the members of the cabbage family can be planted twice in a single season; once in early spring for the summer crop and again in July for a fall crop (see pages 116–21). Bush beans can be planted several times during the season. All these facts should be marked on your plan, and you can even lay it out schematically, putting down on your chart "a row of early carrots followed by beans." Preferably the same crops should not follow each other in exactly the same place, either in a single season or even in consecutive years. Plant disease is apt to appear if a certain piece of ground consistently carries the same crop. Even if this

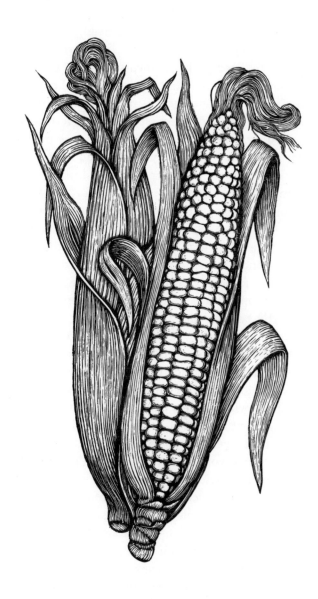

Corn

doesn't happen the quality of the vegetable declines as fertilizers and trace elements in exactly the same proportions are taken steadily from the ground by identical root systems. It is important also to give thought to the height of the plants which you are going to grow, and how far apart they should stand at maturity. Seed packages themselves will provide you with much of this information. It is worth remembering which vegetables can grow where there is not full sunlight all day; peas, if you have room for them, spinach, and lettuce all fall into this category. The latter two are much less inclined to "bolt," that is, run to seed, if they are planted where they do not have full sun. The same principle of choosing leafy, shade-tolerant plants should also be applied as you rough out your planting plan for the rows that are going to be set out beside tall-growing specimens such as broccoli or the plants that you are going to intercrop (that is to say, plant beside slower-growing plants and harvest before the slower-growing plants, such as corn and tomatoes, really begin to spread).

Almost everyone tries to squeeze a few **flowers** into a vegetable plot, partly because they liven it up, but mainly because plants grown this way can be ruthlessly cut for use in the house. Annual flowers do exceptionally well in rows in a well-prepared vegetable plot; in fact, in my experience they do too well and take up too much precious space for too long. I have now given up growing flowers among the vegetables for reasons of space, except for one plant, marigolds. These I still set out at random all over the plot; I use African and French varieties, but I try to avoid those that grow tall or very spreadingly. The reason for having them among the vegetables is that their roots exude a substance that repels root nematodes: those microscopic eellike pests won't trouble a gardener who grows a few marigolds along with the vegetables!

Rhubarb, a perennial which provides much-appreciated spring fruit when very little else fresh exists in the home plot, is too large for most small growing areas. What's more, it has to be left undisturbed each fall, and this makes soil preparation very difficult, not to mention the problem with the area around the roots becoming a weed haven. Rhubarb can better be

grown as a specimen plant elsewhere in the yard. It can also be treated as an ornamental feature of a flower bed, and it need not be allowed to take up space in a vegetable plot. Do not try to incorporate **strawberries** or **asparagus** into a small plot. Both these plants are also perennials. Asparagus, in fact, is extraordinarily long-lived; I have known neglected old beds that still threw up succulent stalks twenty years after they were originally planted.

Both strawberries and asparagus take up a great deal of room on a permanent basis, and though I describe asparagus culture on pages 163–66, I do not consider them suitable for beginning gardeners in a suburban plot. If you have a huge, sunny yard with all the growing space in the world, both these crops are worth planting. The return you get from them is incomparably better than anything that you can buy. But since both will take two full seasons to provide a harvest that is really worthwhile, do make sure that you really enjoy vegetable gardening and mean to go on with it before you undertake the considerable effort that is involved in making asparagus trenches or planting rows of strawberries.

Although the first vegetable plot is inevitably a bit of a gamble, there is no need to fly completely blind. Once you've made out your plan and sent for your seed packages, **read the information on the packages extremely carefully.** It was put there to enable you to avoid some of the more common errors, and you should modify your rough plan according to the instructions you find on these packages. There is one piece of information given on seed packages that is not always entirely understood—the number of days they take to reach maturity. This is a rough estimate of the length of time that plants sown from seed will take in perfect weather to come to harvest, and quite obviously perfect weather does not always exist. If you had a late, cold spring, the time is going to be lengthened. Plants that are grown indoors and set out into warmed-up ground—eggplants, tomatoes, peppers, for example—are often listed by the number of days they will take to reach maturity from the time they go outdoors, not from the time they are sown as seed.

My vegetable gardening activities begin in very early spring when I set about **starting the seeds and the plants that must have a head start** in our cold climate if they are to be worth growing (see pages 135–49). At this time I also check around to see which local growers are also raising, or expect to have available, the same plants, and there's a world of difference in those two situations. Local greenhouses that actually grow their own plants are becoming rare. Most greenhouses and garden centers buy preraised annual and vegetable plants from wholesalers who grow them in enormous quantities. The plants raised by wholesalers often come from slightly warmer areas of the country and are not always as well conditioned to northern growing conditions when they first appear on sale. This can be particularly troublesome when you are buying plants to be set out early. Often wholesale-raised plants are also marketed in the least acceptable form: planted in a single flat or container without any division between the roots of the plants. If you want the best possible plants and vegetables, the local growers who raise their own in individual plots will produce the best buys. But in these days of soaring cost local growers who will go in for this work are scarce, and it is up to us to give them the strongest possible community support. In small communities it is sometimes possible to get a greenhouse to raise plants from the seed packages you have bought. This is by far the best way to get healthy plants that are suited to your particular area, but it usually can be done only if you assure the grower that the plants he raises for you will all be bought. To ensure that, you must enlist the cooperation of vegetable-growing neighbors. It is also only proper that a greenhouse that raises special plants for you be allowed to sell separately, and for its own profit, any extra plants that may be available after you and your friends have bought all you want. But remember, these plans must be made early since the grower has to plan his space and schedule.

The next job is to round up, but keep under cover, all the necessary **planting equipment** that will be needed as soon as it's possible to work outdoors. For me, this includes a couple of long boards the width of our plot to hold the mulch back,

and three or four sharpened stakes that keep each board steady. I also set up a rake, a hoe to make the planting furrows, and a line of strong twine wound around two short, sturdy stakes to keep everything straight. I make a lot of croquet-wicket-like wire hoops out of coat hangers and cut lengths of plastic to put over them to cover planted rows. I put a trowel, a sharpened knife, a plastic spoon, and a small bottle of water-soluble fertilizer in a plastic bucket and add these to the pile together with a watering can. I also find my kneeling pad and put that in the heap. Kneeling pads are not only for your personal comfort, though they make an enormous difference when the ground is still wet, but equally important they prevent you from making a series of deep indentions in the damp spring soil. At this same time I lay in a five-pound bag of a balanced fertilizer high in phosphorus—5-10-5 or 5-10-10 will do—and a five-pound bag of organic fertilizer very high in nitrogen. The latter can be sludge marketed commercially as Milorganite, dried blood, cottonseed meal, or fish meal. Gathering together the materials needed for spring gardening may seem a superfluous gesture while the snow still lies on the ground, but over the long years of vegetable growing I have found it to be a most valuable piece of forethought. Early spring planting time is a tremendously rushed time in garden stores as well as in the yard. Until I forced myself to get organized early and have everything available in one place, I wasted a lot of precious planting weather tracking down vital equipment.

As soon as the frost leaves the ground and the soil dries out somewhat, the preliminary work must start.

> **Soil is ready to work when a handful can be picked up and squeezed together so that it falls apart slowly into large particles when the pressure is released. If the soil stays compressed, it is too wet, and should wait a few more days.**

If the plot was not prepared in the fall, this is the moment when all the activities described in the chapter on soil must be got under way. If the ground was virgin land, or if the vegeta-

bles are to be grown in what was once a flower garden, the
addition of extra fertilizer in the spring will help bring fine
crops. If fertilizer was added in the fall, all you need to do in
the spring is spread the balanced 5-10-5, or what have you,
over the open ground like a dusting of light snow and rake it
in. If you did not fertilize in the fall and do not use a perpetual
mulch and fertility-renewing scheme, spring fertilizing will be
necessary in order to harvest a good crop. If a chemical fertilizer is used, or if lime is added in the spring, the mixture of
fertilizer and lime must be raked into the soil as deeply as
possible, and the ground kept well watered for at least a week
before any seed is sown, unless there have been heavy rains.
The delicate roots of little seedlings can easily be burned. This
is one of the periods when I feel that an organic fertilizer with
the same high phosphorus reading is the wisest choice, but
with organic fertilizer do not forget that where five pounds per
100 square feet will do with a chemical mixture, ten pounds
will be needed with organic material. The value of using organic fertilizer in the spring is that you do not have to wait for
a week before you can plant the seeds, and once I get going
with gardening I hate to have to stop.

Spring Fertilizing
If you are fertilizing for the first time and are using
chemical fertilizer, spread five pounds of 5-10-5 or
5-10-10 for every 100 square feet of land and rake
it in very thoroughly.

Seed Planting

There are some exceedingly **hardy vegetable plants and seeds** that can be got into the ground as soon as the frost leaves it, while it's almost too cold to work outdoors. These hardy characters include all the members of the cabbage family (such as broccoli, cauliflower, and kale) and the onion tribe (garlic bulbs, chives, shallots, and leeks). Spinach seed can also go safely into the cold ground, as can lettuce, parsley, peas, and turnips. I used to do this bitterly cold early planting as soon as the frost left the land, but now I think the return in growth is really not worth the effort. I now wait another two weeks after the mulch has been pulled back until the soil itself has warmed up. I then undertake a big spring planting that includes the hardy plants as well as the seeds of those that are described on most charts as being **semihardy.** These are carrots, beets, Swiss chard, radishes, dill, parsnips, and a very early bush bean called Royalty Purple Pod, which produces stringless purple pods that turn green when cooked.

Purple-pod beans will give you a great jump on the season, since it's the only bean seed I know that can go in cold ground without rotting. The rest of the beans have to wait until the ground is really warmed up, and until there is no chance of air frost. With Purple Pod I put my wicket-like wire hoops over the furrows as I sow the beans and then when the bean

sprouts break through and I hear a sinister weather forecast I rush out and cover the rows with plastic. This gives me a harvest of beans at least two weeks ahead of more conventional sowings of tender green bush beans. For those who have space to grow them, potatoes should also go into the ground at this medium to early planting date.

Plant and seed rows do best if they run from north to south, which eliminates the problem of **tall plants** casting shadows. In the northern tier of states the direction of the rows is not a problem, for the sun is so far north in the summer. But very tall plants, pole beans, corn and tomatoes, and all plants grown on trellises are always better on the northern or western side. A block of space should therefore be left and trellises erected along the outer edges of every plot in these two locations to accommodate these particular plants, none of which can go into the ground at the early planting stage.

How to Grow Specific Vegetables

The exact details of how each plant needs to be grown, the spaces to which it should be thinned, and its fertilizer needs will be found in the material on specific vegetables at the end of the book. The general method by which I plant is the same for everything and will be discussed here.

Among the early plants that will grow tall and therefore throw shade are peas, if you have room for them in your plot. Peas are a cool-weather crop, and they won't last long in the average summer. And regardless of what other books may say, my experience has been that peas, even the so-called bush variety, do better with something to climb on or lean against. Chicken wire with iron pipe 1 inch in diameter threaded

through it and driven firmly into the ground makes an excellent support for peas. Some gardeners support their peas with brush, small branches stuck in the ground. Since peas are such a short-season crop, they need both cool planting and cool growing conditions and will give out as soon as the hot nights set in. For this reason their temporary support system can be set so that it spreads a little over the area where the later tall, hot-weather crops are to grow, for everything connected with peas will be well out of the way before those late plants really get going. Both peas and pole beans, if you're saving space for the latter, are legumes, members of the same family. Rows of peas should, therefore, always be set out beside the area where corn and tomatoes will take up the story later in the season, and not where the pole beans are to grow.

The other rather large-scale early crop is **broccoli,** which, if well grown, gets quite tall. Broccoli will continue to give a good crop of side shoots long after the main head has been cut, until around midsummer. For that reason it should be set on the west side of the plot. A second planting of broccoli is an important vegetable for the fall garden. There is now **purple cauliflower** available that several of my friends have grown. It grows more slowly but calls for less complicated horticultural care than the usual blanched cauliflower. It turns green when cooked and is alleged to have a much more delicate flavor than broccoli, though apparently it tastes a little like it. If you want to raise it in the place of broccoli it does not, of course, take up nearly so much room or throw any shade. On the other hand, it is not as continuously productive as broccoli. So for my money a few plants of broccoli remain an excellent horticultural investment for the gardener with a small plot, particularly since the cabbageworm does not affect the early plantings. Nevertheless, I intend to try the purple-head cauliflower in my garden; used raw it should be a handsome addition to salads.

Spinach, another cool-weather crop that peters out when the weather heats up, and lettuce can both be sown in the most shady area of the plot. Both vegetables tolerate less sun than most. Spinach, incidentally, will soon tell you, if you do not

When to Plant

Hardy	Semihardy	Not Hardy	Hot-Weather
(Plant 4 weeks before air-frost-free date)	(Plant 2 weeks before air-frost-free date)	(Plant on air-frost-free date)	(Plant when night and day temperatures remain over 55°)
Broccoli	Beets	Basil	Beans, lima
Cabbage	Carrots	Beans, green	Cucumbers
Cauliflower	Chard	Corn	Eggplant
Chives	Dill	New Zealand spinach	Melons
Garlic	Mustard		Peppers
Kale	Parsnips		Squash
Leeks	Potatoes		Tomatoes
Lettuce	Beans, purple-pod bush		
Onions	Radishes		
Parsley			
Peas			
Shallots			
Spinach			
Turnips			

test your ground, whether your soil is overacid by the way it develops. If the pH is very low the spinach will do very poorly. It is also possible to make use of the vacant areas that are waiting on the north and west side of your plot for the hot-weather plants by setting out very early rows of spinach and **lettuce** seed during that early, shivering planting period. Both spinach and lettuce are usable when they are quite small. If the weather heats up early and the hot-weather plants expand unexpectedly soon, the rows of spinach and lettuce can be used at a very tender stage. If the weather remains cool, the spinach and lettuce can develop into big plants without interfering

with the hot-weather crops, which will not spread out until the nights are warm.

I'm against the idea I frequently see advocated of growing lettuce between widely spaced plants of cabbage, broccoli, and cauliflower. The cabbage family do, it is true, take time to develop, and in theory it should be perfectly possible to harvest a fine crop of lettuce interspersed among them long before the cabbage and its various relatives begin to take up all the space. But this process, which is called **intercropping,** has, for me, always proved to be something that seems perfectly possible on paper and yet simply does not work. The main crop invariably does poorly, though I do know growers who can pull it off. The problem in our plot may be the perpetual mulch-covered ground which gets a little compacted from all the tramping to and fro setting out and harvesting the lettuce. Because I cannot see the compacted soil I do not loosen it to let in air, something that would happen automatically if I were weeding uncovered ground with a hoe. Perhaps it is the compaction that hinders the development of the long-term plants, and why I have not had success with this style of intercropping. If you have a small plot and want to grow slowly developing plants, such as cabbage, go ahead and try intercropping with quick-growing salad greens or radishes. What fails for me may well work for you, and, if it does work, you will certainly get much more use out of that particular piece of land.

After the lettuce and spinach are harvested, and these are always the first fruits of the labor of the vegetable plot, the area where they grew (except when they were rushed in ahead of long-lasting hot-weather vegetables) should always be put down to root crops in order to change the succession of what the ground is expected to support. All the cabbage family, and **beets** and **carrots** are two-season crops, that is, there should be a later reseeding or replanting in order to provide a full harvest (see pages 116–20). Beets provide a double harvest from a single sowing, since the thinnings can be used as beet greens long before the root itself starts to expand. **Onions** and **Swiss chard** are all-season crops; though onions can, of course, be sown thickly, pulled before they start to swell, and used as scallions.

I try to grow these two near each other so they will not be disturbed when the midsummer replanting takes place.

I use **parsley** in two varieties, and I grow it as an attractive edging where it is easy to reach. Parsley is, however, another vegetable that needs less sun than most, and it can be grown in a shady place in your plot. I've grown **dill** for so long that it tends to pop up all over the lot wherever the mulch is drawn back. This is fine by me, since I cannot get enough of this herb. But dill goes to seed quite fast, and it's wise to reseed every three weeks for an all-season supply. Each year I also scatter expendable dill seed around the area where I intend to set out tomato plants, for the ravenous tomato worm prefers it to tomatoes. **Garlic,** which is also an excellent pest preventative, I set out in cloves or segments of bulbs at random in every row of seed that is planted early in the season. This method spreads the garlic evenly all around the vegetable plot, which is the way I like to grow it. Dating from a rather earlier stage in my vegetable gardening I still have some perennial sage, a tarragon plant, and an uncontrollable Egyptian onion—that strange one that forms its small bulbs on top of the stem instead of at the bottom—along one outer edge of the garden, but now, on the whole, I grow my herbs in containers (see pages 132–34).

I've already stressed that it is important to lay out rows of early vegetables so they don't shade each other, and that those that will ultimately be replaced be near each other. It is equally important to realize that the whole length of any projected row of certain vegetables need not be sown at the same time.

Vegetables that are planted only once during the growing season and develop slowly should have the entire row planted simultaneously; these are the crops like cucumbers, squash, and tomatoes. Vegetables that mature quickly like lettuce, or vegetables that are harvested at different stages in their growth, such as carrots and beets, or vegetables that bear very heavily, like chard and New Zealand spinach, should all be planted in small amounts; a row 6 feet long the first time is quite enough.

Beans

The reason for this is that it's almost impossible to sow seed far enough apart to allow the plants sufficient room to develop properly. Some thinning out of surplus plants inevitably has to be done. If only a portion of the row has been seeded and the rest of the row left covered with mulch, some of the thinnings can usually be carefully lifted and transplanted into the unused portion of the row (page 109). Transplanting is best done in the cool of the evening, but no matter how carefully done, it always slightly checks the growth of a plant. This will delay crop development and will provide you with a staggered harvest with a single sowing.

After there is no danger of frost, though most gardeners take a chance and plant earlier, **green bush snap beans** can be planted. This is the vegetable that is reasonably simple to grow and extremely easy to plant far too heavily. Bush beans do not transplant, but the seed is large enough to make it possible to space the plants properly in the first place. Incidentally, if beans have not appeared within two weeks of being put into the ground, the seed has probably rotted. The soil was either too wet or too cold, and a second batch of seed should be sown. Bush beans must be harvested as soon as the pods reach an edible size. If the first beans are allowed to become enormous the bush will stop producing. Bush beans carry a very heavy crop for about two weeks if the weather is good, and the best way to prevent a dreadful glut and still have a steady supply of this vegetable is, therefore, to sow a short row about every two weeks. After the row of purple-pod beans in early spring, always use the same variety so that the length of time for harvesting is consistent. In this way you will have new beans coming in just as your old crop is over. If, in spite of all these warnings, you too succumb to "bean glut syndrone" let the excess mature and dry on the vine. You can then pick and shell them and store them in jars for use in making a good rich soup in the dead of winter.

Corn can also be planted at the same time that bush beans go into the ground. Corn is one of those vegetables that tastes infinitely better home grown, and there is not a gardener alive who doesn't want to try to raise his own. But corn takes up a

Planting Suggestions

Run rows from north to south to avoid vegetables
shading each other.

Plant tall plants and trellis-grown crops on northern
and western sides of plot.

Plant early crops which will be succeeded by late
crops near each other.

Plant an early-harvest crop of peas, lettuce, and
spinach in the area reserved for hot-weather crops
such as tomatoes, peppers, and eggplant.

Follow early leaf crops with root crops for fall harvesting and early root crops with fall leafy crops.

Avoid planting peas and beans successively in the
same spot.

Avoid planting cabbage, broccoli, cauliflower, kale,
and Brussels sprouts, in the same place each year.

Avoid planting tomatoes, peppers, and eggplant side
by side or where the other has grown previously.

Put in successive small plantings of heavy croppers
such as bush beans.

great deal of space, and since it is also wind pollinated it has
to be planted either in blocks or in three or four short rows side
by side. To extend the harvesting period, you can plant three
kinds of corn, each with a successively later maturation date.
Corn is tremendously affected by the weather: it will not grow
until the nights have warmed up. It is also hard to bring to
successful harvest where raccoons are present, and raccoons
are the wild animals that seem to have adapted themselves best
to suburban life: there is a positive raccoon explosion in almost
every suburb. I will discuss how to handle corn on pages 185–

87, but I must honestly admit that I have now, after many years of growing my own, most reluctantly ceased to raise it. My plot was really not large enough, and the corn was not worth the space it took up for the small amount I was able to harvest.

Gardeners who do grow corn in small plots often justify the space it takes by intercropping. Lettuce or sometimes pumpkins is the plant most often used between the rows of sprouting corn. The Indians grew corn and climbing beans together in the same furrows, harvesting the corn before the beans worked their way far up the corn stems, which provided support without all that business of trellises and poles. This is a worthwhile method of attempting to grow corn in a small plot. The beans can be scarlet runners or Kentucky Wonders, and they should go into the ground in the same furrow as the corn itself, but after the corn has sprouted. You will have a miniature jungle on your hands growing this way, but it is a method of double cropping that can pay off for those who cannot live without corn in their home vegetable plot.

Regardless of how they are grown, I recommend the English version of the **climbing beans,** the scarlet runner, for beginning gardeners. **Scarlet runners** can be grown in a position that does not have full sun. The flowers are like red sweet peas and form a very decorative screen along a wall or trained up wire or string, anywhere that gets partial sun. Scarlet runner beans have now been rehybridized so that the stringy part that used to be rather bothersome has been eliminated. They are profuse croppers over a very long period from about mid-August on, and they are much easier to grow than some of the American varieties. The place where they are to be planted can carry an early crop of spinach, which needs exactly the same conditions of not quite full sun. **Kentucky Wonders** or **Romano Italian pole beans** are also well worth growing; my preference is toward the Romano pole bean, since it comes in earlier and crops all season long. Pole beans need supports, which can be string, netting, or some kind of trellis. Their culture is discussed on page 169.

The last of the seeds that can go directly into the ground after the soil has really warmed up are cucumbers and all the

members of the **squash** family. **Melons, peppers, eggplants, and tomatoes,** the famous hot-weather foursome, are usually set out as prestarted plants. **Cucumbers** take a very short time to mature; in less than two months small cucumbers will be ready to harvest. For me seed sown straight into the ground seems to do better than little transplants. Cucumbers are very amenable to training: they will grow up netting or wire, and they will even scramble about in a hedge, though this makes them hard to harvest. Be sure to arrange them so that they do not throw too much shade on the garden. I usually grow my cucumbers in containers outside my plot, but I have sometimes grown them running about on the ground in spare parts of the garden.They flourish particularly well at the edge of a sunny compost plot. The new gardener can, in fact, be fairly casual about the location of cucumbers.

Squash takes up an enormous amount of space unless the bush type is used. I have ceased to grow squash in anything except containers (pages 124 ff.), and for me they do much better set out as preraised plants. Both cucumbers and squash need a very steady supply of ground moisture, so they are, above all, plants that need heavy mulching. If you do not mulch your garden and expect to be away during the early part of the summer you must realize that both your squash and your cucumbers will simply stand still and cease to develop until they receive a steady supply of moisture once more. And if the crop is not picked when it is ready the plants will cease to bear.

Midsummer usually finds a great dearth of greens for salads in the average plot, for hot air is too much for both spinach and lettuce. This is the time when **Swiss chard** sown earlier in the season comes into its own. To provide a change from unending chard a row of **New Zealand spinach,** which is not in fact true spinach, should be sown in the warmed-up ground at the same time the beans and corn go in. New Zealand spinach is slow to germinate and takes up rather more room than I like. Because of this slow germination and the appalling weeds that spring up where I have to leave the ground unmulched waiting for the seedlings to appear, I have taken to starting New Zealand spinach indoors, just as I do my tomatoes and eggplants.

It transplants perfectly easily and spreads a considerable width as it grows, providing you with edible leaves and tips throughout the hottest weather. Furthermore, once you have got New Zealand spinach in your garden you will have it forever, particularly if you do not mulch your ground. It is a great self-seeder, and the ground where the row was last year will almost inevitably produce volunteer seedlings as the weather warms up. These can be very easily transplanted into a new place. There is a climbing variety (also not a true spinach) called **Malabar spinach,** which I have seen very enthusiastically described in gardening magazines and seed catalogs. I have never grown it myself, but I understand that it too can take hot weather. For people in hot areas who find themselves running very short of summer greens this is a plant that obviously would be worth trying.

The actual process of **sowing seed** is fairly simple. Straight rows always look much better than wavy ones and can be produced by drawing a twine line taut between two stakes and wrapping it around the bottom of the stake so that the line rests on the ground. If you make the first row parallel with the outside of the plot the rest will follow suit. Small seeds in the spring need only a very shallow furrow, something around half an inch deep.

The handle of a hoe pressed lightly into the ground makes a seed bed of just about the right depth for small seeds. But always check the information on your seed packet.

Every gardener has his own way of distributing seed down a furrow. I have never had any luck shaking it straight from the corner of the package; with me this invariably results in nothing or a deluge. Nor have I done well with the gadgets sold for the purpose of distributing seed evenly. My method is to pour some seed into the palm of my left hand, which must be dry so that any leftover seed will not be damp, and to sow this pinch by pinch, rubbing it between the thumb and the first finger of my right hand. Once a pinch of seed is in the furrow, I separate it with a sharpened pencil point.

Spring Seed Sowing

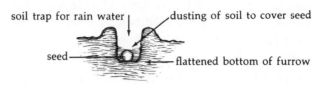

soil trap for rain water   dusting of soil to cover seed

seed ——————— flattened bottom of furrow

How far apart to sow seed is a tough problem, and I will deal with it under the specific plants at the end of the book.

Until you are very sure of what you're about, I would suggest you sow fairly thickly and then try to twitch each tiny seed about half an inch apart. Larger seed should stand an inch apart.

Beet and chard seeds, which are in fact several seeds in one, should be sown at least three inches apart, since each seed yields a little clump of plants.

For good germination seeds should never be covered too deeply.

If you consider how a seed in the wild falls on top of the ground and then turns into a triumphant, thick weed, this fact becomes self-evident. Fine seeds should not have more than a dusting of soil on top of them. Larger seeds, which are sown in a furrow about an inch deep, should be covered more deeply, but, large or small, seeds should in the spring have only enough earth put on top of them to hide them from view, shade them from the sun, and maintain an evenly moist condition. Leave the earth mounded up on both sides of any planted row. The mounds trap rain water, and moisture is tremendously important for good seed germination. They also shield the emerging shoots from bitter wind.

What is extremely important in sowing seed is to

make sure that the seed lies in close contact both with the soil above and with the soil below.

It is wise also to remember that all seed germinates better on a firm, even surface. If you sow fine seed in a furrow made by

pressing a hoe handle in the ground, the seed bed will be curved, not flat; if the furrow is made by a hoe it will be V-shaped. I flatten the seed bed by thumping the depression with the back of the hoe before sowing the seed, and again after the seed has been covered with soil or vermiculite. This double flattening process, which makes sure that the seed lies on even ground and is in contact with the earth over and under it, is just as important for big seed as it is for small.

The earth into which seed is to go should be neither too wet nor too dry.

This, I realize, is the kind of statement that infuriates new gardeners, but it's very difficult to be more precise. Soil that cannot pass the squeeze test (page 81) because there have been weeks of heavy rain should be allowed to dry out a little before seed is sown, no matter how warm the weather. If soil looks powdery and dry, the furrow should be well moistened the evening before the seed goes in. If the weather seems unseasonably hot and dry or very windy when the first fine seeds are sown and the garden soil is clay with a tendency to cake, then the gardener will be wise to fill the furrow with vermiculite, which remains soft and retains moisture much better than earth and will not hinder the little seeds from breaking through by forming a hard crust. Mulch cannot be put down over emerging seeds (it will smother them just as it smothers weeds). It is possible to conserve moisture in rows where seed has just been sown by spreading bone-dry soil that has been scraped up from another part of the yard over the dampened earth until nothing moist remains to be seen. The powdery dry soil in itself serves as a water-conserving mulch. If you intend to water the rows where seed has been sown until the plants break through, do this job by hand with a watering can that has a fine rose on the end of the spout. (A rose is a water diffuser that breaks the force of the stream rushing through.) Watering newly seeded rows or tiny germinating plants with a hose usually washes them right out of the ground. The only way a hose can be used is with a mister attachment at the business end.

Since the earth ridges on each side of the row mark where seed has been sown, I do not find it necessary to sow radishes among the slow-germinating seeds in order to know where my planted areas lie. But since as a family we're not very keen on radishes, it may be that I am slow to bother with them at any time. For those who enjoy radishes, a few seeds sprinkled alongside whatever is the main crop will enable the gardener to grow radishes and **mark the place where seed has been sown.** The old-fashioned method of sticking the empty seed package through a stick at one end of the planted row is not suitable if you're going to sow only a short section at a time, for the remaining seed should be saved. And even if you've used it all up, this is a highly undesirable way of marking what you have sown, as the paper package inevitably gets blown away! If you want to mark your row, buy painted or plastic labels and write on them with one of the indelible pencils sold for that purpose.

I also do not follow the practice of **block sowing,** which I frequently see advised for carrots and for lettuce. Block sowing means sprinkling seed all over a squared-out area. I tried this once, and the problem of thinning, not to mention weeding and mulching, put me off this way of growing plants forever.

Carrots, parsley, and parsnips all take a very long time to germinate, and when the first green wisps appear above ground there are, at least in my garden, often horrible gaps. I have had quick, thick, even germination with all these closely related plants by pouring **boiling water** straight from the kettle over the seed once it is on the ground before the earth is drawn back down over it. The boiling water ensures and hastens the softening of the seed coat. Do try this method—you'll be surprised at the results, just as long as you remember that the water you use must be boiling hot.

Where the vegetable plot is on a **clay soil** or in a **dampish place,** raised beds are best for beets and carrots, which do not germinate well in overwet soil. Neither beets nor carrots need a tremendous amount of space between the rows. What is much more important for their good root development is a deep topsoil, rich in organic matter, particularly compost, and

free of stones. I have had better crops of both these root vegetables, and had them take up much less garden space, since I
took to planting two short rows of the same plant side by side
less than 10 inches apart.

Certain vegetables are sometimes planted not in rows but
in clumps or groups, which are called "**hills**" by horticulturists.
Hills consist of several seeds sown close together but a considerable distance from the next group in the row; the term does
not necessarily mean a mound of earth. With hill planting five
or six seeds are planted close together on a flat surface an inch
below soil level; the seeds are then covered with soil and firmed
down in the usual manner. After germination the seedlings are
reduced to the three strongest specimens that are the farthest
away from each other. Cucumbers, squash, and melons that
will be allowed to trail along the ground are sometimes planted
in hills in big yards. Corn, being wind pollinated, used always
to be planted this way in order to be sure that each plant was
in close contact with another. Corn is still occasionally planted
in hills, even in small plots. For those who want to try this style
of growing, the preparation of hills for different plants is described in detail in the section dealing with specific plants.

**In a small plot it is sometimes almost impossible
not to put the same crop in the same place in consecutive years, particularly if succession planting is
practiced, that is, a second, midsummer sowing is
made for a fall crop.**

My growing area is small enough to make it impossible for me
always to vary what I grow where each year. And though I try
to change the positions, I don't worry too much about it. The
tremendous amount of organic matter that slowly incorporates
itself into the soil from our perpetual mulch seems to take care
of the problem. Vegetable gardening takes quite enough time
and energy without the gardener's worrying about everything,
so if certain positions seem best for specific crops year after
year, I go right ahead and grow them in the same place. But I
don't think this method would be successful, as it has been,
without the huge amount of organic matter we use. This is a

point which I must make very clear with regard to my rather casual attitude, for it has now been fairly clearly proven that large quantities of organic matter added regularly to the soil serve as a buffer against various soil diseases. I do, however, take pains to alternate leafy and root crops whenever I am using the same furrow, or ground very close by, for a second planting in a single season. Too much of one type of nutrient —nitrogen, for example, with the leafy plants, or phosphorus with a root crop—will have been taken from the soil for a second similar crop to be grown in the same place in the same season.

Another exception to my rather casual ways are the brassicas, or the cabbage family. I shift cabbage, broccoli, cauliflower, kale, Brussels sprouts, and mustard to totally new areas each year, bearing in mind as I change their position the shade the broccoli may cast. I do this because of a disease known as **clubfoot** that can affect all members of the cabbage family. Clubfoot, once in the soil, lasts a very long time and makes it impossible to raise any of that family in or near the affected area for many years. To date my ground has been spared this affliction, and I hope to keep it out by being very careful to grow the broccoli in a different locality each year. And this is where my long-term planting charts, rough as they are, serve a very useful purpose. It is extraordinarily difficult to remember two years later where you had that row of cabbage unless you put it down at the time. I shall be dealing with other soil pests in greater detail in a later section.

Setting Out Plants

Setting out **preraised plants** in a vegetable plot, whether they've been home raised (pages 135–49) or bought from a commercial outlet, is not a difficult job, but it should follow some predetermined rules so that the little plants will not suffer a setback as a result of their change of life style. Plants that are once badly checked in their growth never will produce optimum crops. If you have a choice among nurserymen who have prestarted vegetables for sale in your area, make a point of patronizing those who've raised each plant in an individual container. These containers can be square peat pots or peat pellets crammed into a little box or flat, as it is usually called. Containers can also be flats that are sectioned off with dividers into separate compartments rather like an ice tray. Plants sold this way are inclined to be rather expensive, since the flat and divider are often made of a long-lasting material called Tufflite, whose cost is added to the charge for the plants. I find Tufflite flats a useful investment, since they are everlasting, and I use them year after year for my own home-grown windowsill plants.

If all this seems too expensive, look for plants that are sold in paper-thin molded plastic flats with four separate compartments for the root systems of the plants they contain. These little flats are also worth keeping for home use another year,

for, being square, they fit easily onto a tray on a sunny windowsill. My only complaint about them is that they contain
only four plants; old-fashioned flats always contained six,
which was just the right amount for the average small plot.
Four is too little, if you are realistic enough to plan for possible
disasters, while eight is often too many. If possible, avoid
buying prestarted plants that are growing in a solid block of
soil, even though these will be cheaper.

Reputable garden centers will not offer prestarted plants
for sale unless or until they're completely conditioned to go
straight into the ground in the area where they are being sold.
This is why it is unwise to buy prestarted plants by mail or
from a nursery in some other area than your own where you
have to drive a tremendous distance to get there. The climate
may be just that much colder or warmer than yours to make
such purchases unhappy in your ground. Another important
reason for buying plants locally is to be able to check on their
condition before you hand over your money. This is extremely
important not only because the health of the tiny plant will
have a direct bearing on the crop it ultimately will bear (a
sickly seedling never really develops properly), but also in
order to prevent plant disease from being brought onto your
land through diseased stock.

The problem of **clubfoot** on the cabbage family almost
always arises in the first place from an infected plant, and this
you will not be able to see while the seedling is still in the pot.
When you buy cabbage or broccoli plants it is always wise to
wash the soil off the root system in lukewarm water and make
sure there is no suspicious look to the roots before you plant
them in your clean soil. If the roots are swollen or distorted,
the name of the disease indicates what you have to look for,
put any brassica plants you have just bought at that particular
store, and the soil in which they are growing, into large plastic
garbage bags, seal these up, and send them out with the trash.
Never consign suspicious plant material of this family, or the
soil that has been around their roots, to your compost pile.

Store-bought plants should be short and sturdy; their
stems should be thick, and the color of the leaves a good dark

Plant Purchasing and Storage Tips

Buy plants locally.

Choose plants raised in individual containers.

Look for short, sturdy, thick-stemmed, dark green
plants.

Check for strong, white roots.

Look at underside of leaves and check carefully
for signs of plant pests and diseases.

Store plants outdoors, in a bright place out of the
wind and sun, and slightly on the dry side.

Water plants thoroughly at least two hours before
they are planted.

Get purchased plants into the ground as soon as
possible.

green. Avoid plants that have grown tall and thin; these may look further developed, but they are, in fact, a poor purchase. A tall thin seedling will have outgrown the food supply in the small pot, and the roots may have suffered permanent damage. Long, lanky growth also suggests that the plant has not had enough light at a vital stage in its development. If the plants are offered for sale individually in small peat pots, check the pots. There should be strong, white roots just peeping through the moist sides of these peat containers, not withered, dried-out roots. Do not buy plants with any yellowed or dead leaves. This can be a sign of root damage or that there has been a lack of water at some stage; this again produces a disruption from which the plant will never entirely recover. Avoid plants with curled, rolled, or mottled leaves, or leaves that are flecked with yellow. These all could be harmless symptoms of a temporary nature, but they could also be signs of plant disease, which have no place being deliberately imported onto your land.

Turn the pots upside down so that you can see the under-side of the leaves, and look out for any egg masses, little clusters of white and yellow objects stuck on the back of the leaves. Check for aphids, those green things that cluster along the tips of plants, and, above all, for signs of white fly. White flies are tiny white flecks that rise up when a plant is shifted. It is particularly important to check for white fly on prestarted cucumbers, all the squash family plants, and also tomatoes and eggplants when you come to buy these a little later in the season. Another suspicious sign are pinhead-sized holes in plant leaves, for these may come from the flea beetle. Plant dealers do not knowingly sell diseased or infected plants, but plant pests and diseases appear apparently from nowhere wher-ever large stands of little plants are set out for display over a period of several weeks. That is why it is important to know what you are looking for. It is also the reason why the ground should be ready for the little plants to be set out as soon as they become available, for the shorter the time they are out of the ground the better they will do for you.

After you bring your purchases home, put them in a bright place out of doors out of the wind, and don't drown them with enormous torrents of water if there's to be delay in getting them planted. Transplants are less likely to suffer when they go into the ground if they've been toughened up a little in advance by being kept slightly on the dry side. Don't, how-ever, go to the other extreme and let the plants dry out so much that they wilt, for this misfortune can check their growth for many subsequent weeks. Prestarted plants should have a thorough watering at least two hours before they are to go into the ground.

The **planting process** is exactly the same as planting a shrub or a tree on a miniature scale. Mark the row with a taut string, haul back the mulch, and use a shovel to dig a hole. You don't need to go down to China or to make the hole enor-mously wide, but a cavity a great deal bigger than the root ball you're about to put into it will lead not only to a fast recovery but also to much better long-term growth. The less thorough the preparation of the soil itself in advance, the larger that hole should be. If possible choose an overcast or even a drizzly day

for doing the actual planting-out job, and dig all the holes first. The distance apart for various plants will be found in the section on growing specific vegetables at the end of the book.

In heavy soil, compost at the bottom of the hole and mixed with the soil with which you're going to backfill will give plant roots a better chance of doing well.

Prestarted plants almost invariably have been raised in a very light soil mixture or even in soilless mixes, and the roots of a transplant that is used to such light soil have a very hard time adjusting themselves to heavy clay soil suddenly surrounding them. If you do not have compost to lighten up a clay soil, buy some ready-mix soil at the garden center and lighten your backfill material with that. In very sandy soil half-decomposed compost or damp peat moss can be put at the lowest level of the hole to serve as a water sponge, which will be a great help to the roots as they develop. When the organic matter is in, fill the hole three-quarters of the way up, firming the material down with your fist.

When the holes are ready pop each little plant out of its separate compartment, if you bought them in divided plastic flats.

Rest the root mass on the bottom of the hole, fill in around it, and firm the soil down. With newly set-out transplants it is permissible to put a little bit of the stem below the soil level. When you transplant, take along with you a watering can filled with lukewarm water and the appropriate amount of water-soluble fertilizer dissolved in it. I use the fertilizer in the proportions suggested for starter mixes or transplanting solutions: about a cupful to each plant, pouring the mixture over the foliage of the plant down into the original root ball, after I have firmed the plant in.

If the prestarted plants are in peat pots, stand them in an inch or two of lukewarm water until the peat changes color. This will soften up the sides of the peat, which otherwise can be as

Peas

hard as concrete, but beware of soaking them so long that they begin to disintegrate. Peat pots that have dried out in any way will not crumble up when put into the ground, with a lamentable effect upon the plant roots, which then find themselves permanently enclosed in a kind of cardboard strait jacket. Always break the tops off peat pots so that the sides are exactly level with the soil surface inside them. If a water-soaked peat pot has not yet had roots penetrate through it, peel the pot off too. Also be sure that the top of any peat pot is always completely covered with the earth backfill. If the sides of these pots stick up above the ground into the open air they act as a wick and take water away from the plant roots, and you will get poor growth.

Unlike almost every other horticultural writer, I dislike the **jiffy compressed peat wafers** enclosed in plastic netting that expand when put into warm water. If you buy plants raised in these little circular self-contained peat pots they, too, must be soaked in warm water before planting, and once they are put onto the soil surface the netting should be cut on both sides with sharp scissors. Plastic netting does not disintegrate, and unless it is cut open and at least an inch of soil is put over the top of the pots I have found that the little circular containers

often rise, with the peat bone-dry inside them, above the surface of the garden later in the season, and that the roots of the plant have never really escaped from them. There are also on the market compressed peat pellets without netting; these are made from long fibers and are completely biodegradable.

If you cannot find plants in individual containers and have to buy them **planted in a flat,** then the planting methods are slightly different. Look for all the same problems before you bring the flat home, including dried roots protruding from the vent hole of the flat, which is an indication that the plants have been in their flat too long. Look also for yellowed lower leaves, since this means the smaller plants have been deprived of sufficient light. In most flats one plant is small and stunted; perfection in all six (which these solid flats usually contain) is rather rare. This is something which should not worry the purchaser too much, unless there is rotted tissue showing in the weak plant. In that case, reject the flat.

When the planting holes are ready for your flat of plants, take a very sharp knife and cut down one side of the container if it's of the heavy fiber type. If the flat is plastic you'll have to try cutting away the plastic side, which can be perfectly well done with sharp tin snips. If by chance you've bought plants in an old-fashioned wooden flat, carefully detach one wooden side of the flat. It's hard to knock a flat of plants out in the way that a potted plant can be treated. If there seems no other solution, it can be done by spreading the fingers between the plants as far as you can stretch and then upending the flat very carefully onto one side, sliding the flat out from under and lowering the root mass down again. If you can cut the side out it's far simpler just to slide the whole root mass out intact.

Once out of the flat the soil block full of tangled roots should be put on a hard surface—a board will do. Then take the knife and cut between the rows of plants crosswise and then lengthwise; cut firmly and fast. The more decisively you act with the knife, the less lasting the root damage.

Plants recover fast from a clean cut, whereas sawing at roots

with a blunt knife or, worse still, clippers will produce a trauma from which a root system may never recover.

Plant as before, but avoid pressing down too hard on the injured roots. They should come into contact with the soil but not be pounded into place. It is also better to dilute the starter fertilizer solution before applying it to plants that have had their roots cut. Use half the recommended amount at planting time, and give a second dose a week later over the foliage and down into the root system of the transplants.

It is always a good idea to bury the stem of all transplants a little deeper than they grew originally, and this holds particularly true of transplants with root damage.

Shading may well be needed for all transplants if the weather turns hot.

Dappled, moving shade is the best, and this can be done by sticking branches of brush, or evergreen branches in the ground. Water is particularly important for transplants that have had the traumatic treatment of being cut apart, but be careful not to wash them out of the soil: just see that the earth around them remains moist.

All transplants particularly appreciate a light misting of their foliage early in the morning if the weather is hot.

Water on the foliage early in the morning may get them through the next day's hot weather without wilting, which is a very debilitating process for new, young plants.

Digging a good-sized hole where small plants are to be set does more than just prepare the ground; it also gives you a chance to find any cutworms that may be lurking just under the surface of the soil in that vicinity. In fact, any large, fat grub you discover should be promptly trodden upon and killed, for if it's not a cutworm it may be the grub stage of the Japanese beetle. Many years ago we used to put low tarpaper collars around the plants that were set out early to save them

from cutworms, which work at night and under cold, damp conditions to chew through small juicy stems. Today, even better **plant protectors** can be made from a paper cup with the bottom cut out, or sections of waxed milk cartons will do. They not only protect the young plants from cutworms, but also shelter them against cold wind, which can be a great enemy to even the hardiest little plant when it's first set out. Push the protector, whatever it is, about an inch below surface level. **Cutworms** do not work deep in the ground. I vary what I use according to the size of the plant itself. Once the plants start to expand and have obviously settled in I trim down the high sides of any protector with scissors, but I usually leave the collar in place. It does no harm, and it may be still serving its purpose as a cutworm deterrent. If you didn't take this precaution and subsequently find your plants toppled off with the stems chewed right through, dig down beside each ruined plant as far as 6 inches out from where it once stood. Somewhere beside one of those ruined plants is the offender, and sometimes there is more than one in very cold, damp soil conditions, so check beside each toppled plant. By exterminating them when you have a very good idea of where they are, the plot can usually be cleared of these nuisances, for the first plants they attack will always be individual transplants. If you replant without finding the cutworm your second planting is likely to be attacked. Worse still, emboldened by their success, cutworms sometimes move on from individual plants to devouring sections of newly emerging beets and carrots.

Apart from the professional or home-raised prestarted plants many gardeners also use little plants they thin from rows of seed sown too thickly in the first place. **Transplanting little plants during a thinning operation** is not quite the same thing as setting out preraised plants. For one thing, the roots of the lifted seedlings will be all tangled together, and the operation that has subsequently to be undertaken is called **bare-root planting.** To do this kind of planting you again mark the extension of the row with a line. For tools you need a trowel, a thin spatula or a putty knife, a watering can with water-soluble fertilizer starter solution in it, and two plastic

basins, one piled high with homemade compost or store-bought sterile soil, and the other containing a little warm water.

> **Water the row, and then, using either the spatula or the putty knife, lift a pinch of seedlings, roots, earth, and all, out of the ground, leaving sturdy, individual plants untouched in the row an inch apart. As the clumps of thinnings come up dump them, with all the earth still on their roots, into the warm water in the plastic bowl. Then fill in the open space left in the row with soil from the spare bowl.**

This is fiddling work, and the best way to do it is to have a kneeling plank, which is a long board entirely free of splinters laid down beside the length of the row. With a kneeling board you can scuffle your way along, without having to get up and shift a pad every time. You also need a calm mind and plenty of spare time when you are doing a thinning, transplanting job!

When the whole row has been thinned move the kneeling plank beside the unplanted extension of the row or a fresh unused portion of your plot.

> **Then, with either your fingers or a sharp pointed pencil, carefully disentangle the roots of one of the largest of the thinnings. With one hand, hold the plant by the foliage, never by the stem, for that contains the growing point. With a pencil held in the other hand, free the roots from all the other roots it's been mixed up with. The roots will be covered with wet, slimy muck, which is just what you need, for this protects them from being dried out. Still holding the thinning, with the roots dangling in a miserable tangle, cut a slot in the soil alongside the line with a trowel, lower the plant in, and push the earth back. No transplant should be less than 2 inches apart. Consult the seed packet.**

Choosing and separating the strongest thinnings is by far the most tiresome part of the job; the actual planting is a snap.

After the plants are in, I put a thin layer of mulch over the soil around them. Since most of the transplants have very muddy foliage when they go into the ground, the next step is to water this off and also water around their roots with the starter solution.

I take the same precautions against cutworms as I do with the earlier transplants, but I usually use rather taller protectors, in this case a half-gallon waxed milk carton. The tall sides provide some shade for the little seedling, and they also protect it against wind; the open top prevents any great heat buildup.

It is possible to give transplants a **humid atmosphere,** which will speed their recovery, by putting curved wires that look like croquet wickets across the newly planted rows and covering these with a long sheet of plastic. And if cold damp weather follows hard on the heels of early transplanting this temporary plastic cover can be very helpful. The great danger with plastic protection is the heat of the sun early in the morning, which can do immense damage to tender plants. For this reason you should erect the plastic tunnel in short sections and leave both ends open; even so you must be prepared to whisk the plastic off if there is a buildup of heat and humidity—all the more likely as spring becomes summer. But whatever devices are used as covering material for any sort of plants during the period when the weather by day can become suddenly extremely hot, constant vigilance is called for.

After I've set out the first thinnings, I take the little seedlings that remain and wash them off in clean water. I choose a dozen of the biggest specimens of each variety and put these in baby food jars with only the roots in water; the tops by this time should be given a chance to dry off. I set these in bright light but not in full sun, usually on one of our outdoor plant stands. I watch my planting rows, and if I see a transplant in obvious trouble, I replace it immediately with one from the reserve supply. A transplant in trouble is one that lies flat on the ground and does not revive after a cool night. This is the one period in my vegetable growing when I also go daily up and down the rows of transplants with a watering can in hand.

Nothing is likely to be more fatal at this stage to newly transplanted seedlings than not enough moisture, both at their roots
and on their foliage. Transplants show when they've taken
hold again by turning a stronger color and having generally a
more robust look. Lettuce, chard, and New Zealand spinach
usually come through completely successfully; beets, being
taprooted plants, are more of a gamble; carrots are very difficult
to move, and I find that planting additional seed works better.

**When the weather has entirely warmed up and the
nights as well as the days remain over 55 degrees,
prestarted pepper, eggplant, and tomato plants can
go out.**

Eggplant, peppers, and tomatoes are mildly antipathetic to
each other, so the rows should not be side by side, nor should
they be planted in subsequent years where the others have
grown previously. To ensure success be sure to buy prestarted
peppers and eggplant in individual containers, for these plants
need strong, undisturbed roots at planting-out time. The process of setting them out is exactly the same as has already been
described, but since these are all plants that bear heavily over
a long season, don't go overboard on the number you put in
your plot. **Peppers** and **eggplants** grow large in rich soil. Mine
were constantly toppled by wind, and the crops spoiled by
falling on the ground, until I learned to stake them from the
start. I now put in a stout stake, driven deeply into the ground,
before the plant is set out; staking a growing plant invariably
results in root damage. The little plant itself is set on the south
side of the stake and tied loosely to the support as it develops.

Tomatoes, which are plants that everybody wants to grow
in the home plot, throw some of the deepest roots of any
vegetables. They also are stem rooters, so buried lengths of
stem will throw anchoring roots that will support the plant and
also send up extra nourishment.

**Tomatoes should be buried deeply in a well-pre-
pared hole that has had extra fertilizer high in phosphorus put into its lowest levels. The little plant**

should be set into the soil right up to the first set of true leaves.

If the tomato plant is already tall and leggy it can be set out on its side with the long stem buried and just a tuft of leaves protruding. The leaves will soon straighten, and the plant grow upright. Tomatoes will grow in less than full sun, but the crop will be reduced in quantity and come late. If that is your only position, perhaps you should plant plenty of tomatoes. If, however, you have a good, sunny place for tomatoes and are able to provide the deep, rich soil the roots require, go easy on the number of plants you set out. Next to beans, tomatoes are the plant that tends to glut the most profusely in the home plot. Tomatoes can be allowed to sprawl on the ground, but this way they demand a lot of room, and also much of the fruit gets spoiled lying on wet soil. Tomatoes in home plots are better grown vertically or in containers. The various ways of achieving this are discussed in the section on their specific culture, page 224.

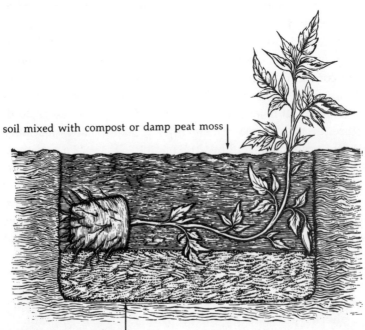

soil mixed with compost or damp peat moss |

compost and phosphate |

Midseason and Late Planting and Care

After the vegetables that need hot nights are set out there is a slight pause in the planting rhythm of the garden—except, of course, for the fortnightly planting of short rows of bush beans and corn, and the reseeding of lettuce, which in midsummer should always be done in the shadiest place the plot possesses. I suggest that this temporary pause be used to get the plants and the ground ready for whatever vagaries the summer weather may bring. **Lay down extra mulches** of grass clippings between every row of planted vegetables, and draw them as close to the top growth as possible. Spread mulch particularly thickly around the cucumbers, melons, tomatoes, eggplants, and peppers. No matter how these are handled, they are all plants that need a regular supply of moisture at their roots at every stage to develop properly. The trick to their successful culture is not to swamp them with water at irregular intervals but to make sure that the surrounding soil is always pleasantly damp, and the only way I know to be certain of this without overwatering is to use a heavy mulch. Most rows of seeded plants also need a **second thinning** in early summer, and at this stage the thinnings should be large enough to be edible.

While thinning or pulling weeds out of a row of carrots, always have extra soil or compost in a bucket beside you to

cover the tops of any carrots that may have been exposed to the light. This prevents them from turning green. When I thin I also weed. Weeds, which are anything—no matter how lovely—growing in an inappropriate place, are a great nuisance in rows of vegetables; they steal moisture and nutrients, and they can grow exuberantly enough to shade the growth of the crop itself. Hand weeding on your knees is the answer, unless, of course, you are gardening in raised beds or in containers. It is impossible to mulch in a close row of plants except rather lightly, but, with the final thinning, a light grass mulch can sometimes be got between the plants that are now far enough apart for full development. For those who do not garden under mulch, weeding has, of course, been the order of the day from the moment the first seeds went in. **Keeping weeds suppressed** is a perpetual chore that is vital for the good health of the plot, even apart from its appearance. But the job is not all that simple, and this perhaps is the proper place to describe how it should be done.

Vegetables in general have a very shallow root system; that is why it is possible to raise most vegetables even on land that does not have deep topsoil.

Because their roots are set close to the surface, vegetables are easily damaged by deep hoeing. The soil should not be disturbed deeper than about an inch.

This is true whether the hoeing takes place beside the furrows or even some distance from them, since vegetables, particularly in poor soils, send out a far-ranging root system. To avoid root damage, don't use the conventional hoe that is useful for making planting furrows; this often goes into the ground too deeply and will do harm, particularly in the hands of a new gardener.

Use a scuffle hoe that lies flat on the surface of the ground and will chop off weeds at ground level both when pushed forward and when pulled back.

The other type of hoe works only when you drag it toward you. Beheading weeds with a flat hoe does not always kill

them: sometimes they resprout. It does, however, avoid damaging the roots of the vegetables. If you go regularly along the rows of your plot beheading the weeds, even tough characters that resprout after this treatment will never have a chance to grow large enough to be a nuisance.

The best time for weeding is unfortunately during the heat of the day, when exposed roots will be killed by the hot sun.

Weeds uprooted in the cool of the evening may recover and start to grow again. If you can weed only after you get home in the evening, picking up the debris is mandatory.

Crabgrass is one of the worst offenders from midseason on, for the growing conditions of a vegetable garden are exactly what suit this nuisance the best. Crabgrass can become almost uncontrollable in an unmulched garden unless it is eliminated regularly, at least once a week. If it turns into large sprawling tufts it will have to be hacked out by hand. Do not let crabgrass get established in rows of root vegetables. Once in, it will seize the space into which the roots are expected to expand and do damage to their development. Crabgrass loves sunlight and light sprinklings of water. In unmulched vegetable gardens crabgrass will not do well if the crops are so thick and successful that they shade the ground, for crabgrass cannot tolerate shade. If watering is done on a regular basis and rather heavily this will also deter crabgrass. Purslane is another pest in a vegetable plot in which the soil is exposed, but this fortunately is a plant that can be uprooted very easily. However, it is also the plant that will reroot if given half a chance!

Do not work among rows of vegetables, either weeding or mulching, after a rain while the foliage is still wet.

Knocking against wet leaves, particularly those of bush beans, can lead to disease, while tramping about on wet soil compacts it and drives out the air.

If the ground was adequately prepared in the fall and refertilized in the spring, I have never found it necessary to fertilize

the early crops that I expect to harvest before early July. I often read recommendations for fertilizing plants in late June by a method known as **side dressing,** which means making a furrow on each side of a row of early vegetables and 4 inches away from the plants themselves, and pouring in specific amounts of dry fertilizer before pulling earth back over the newly opened furrows.

I consider that side dressing should be done only if the plants are obviously doing very poorly, and if a soil test shows a nutrient deficiency.

Extra fertilizer provided automatically at this period in the growing season of a vegetable plot can overfeed the plants. Overfed plants are large, tasteless, and flabby, and much more prone to disease, while the fertilizer that produces this condition is expensive. We grow vegetables for better taste and to eat them at less cost than buying them from a supermarket. Unnecessary fertilizer will ruin both those ambitions. In the plant lists at the end of the book will be found the amount of fertilizer that can be put into the ground beside the growing plants if soil tests show it to be needed, or where there is obviously miserable growth of the plants, but this should not be done automatically and without thought. Poor growth very easily can be the result of bad weather. New gardeners would be well advised to wait through the first growing season and judge how the crops do without this extra stimulant; nine times out of ten if the land was well prepared in the first place (and unless you long for mammoth vegetables) you will find it is not needed.

When the weather starts to really warm up (about late June, for me) the peas, spinach, early lettuce, and turnips are through, and the beets and carrots will be reaching harvestable stage.

As soon as any row or section of a row of vegetables is done, all the debris should be carted away to the compost pile, the ground should be weeded, this time with the garden hoe, and a 2-inch layer of fresh

compost should be laid on top of the area where the crop was harvested. If no compost is available, rake in a couple of inches of damp peat moss. In soils that are not overrich or very deep, or where compost is not available, this is the time to use a balanced fertilizer—10-10-10 is excellent—at the rate of one pound for every 25 feet of row that is being got ready for a second crop.

If compost is also being used, use one-quarter pound of fertilizer for a 25-foot row. Rake this into the top inch of soil, and then water the ground thoroughly. Cover the ground with mulch or even with thick layers of newspapers (anything to keep the weeds out and the soil moist), and leave it for a week so that the fertilizer has time to blend into the soil. If an organic fertilizer is used twice as much will be needed, but there will be no need to wait before planting. You can also use slow-release fertilizers with a high phosphorus content. Though expensive, they work wonderfully well when plenty of organic matter is available. One-half cup of such a fertilizer to a 25-foot row will suffice for a second crop.

Midseason seed is sown exactly like early seed, except that the planting furrow should be considerably deeper and not completely filled in afterward: 2 inches deep for fine seed and 4 inches deep for big seed.

The great danger with midseason sowing is that the seeds will not be able to germinate in dry soil, or that they will rot away or be washed out because the anxious grower overwaters to avoid this very problem! There is also the danger that the soil may cake, and the seedlings won't be able to break through; and that, when and if they get that far, blazing sun or hot summer wind will kill them in short order. Nothing very much can be done about the sun and wind on the surface of the soil; I have not found that shading the row makes much difference. The deep furrow will, however, help, since the germination of the seed takes place lower than usual in the ground in a narrow area fully protected from wind into which the sun's rays can-

Midseason Seed Sowing

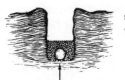

seed covered
with vermiculite

flattened bottom of furrow

additional vermiculite
covering sprouted seed

furrow:
2 in. deep for small seeds   4 in. deep for large seeds

not penetrate very easily. With midseason planting I level the
ground at the bottom of the furrow that is to receive the seed
with the back of a single finger in order to keep the gully very
narrow. The problem of washing out the seed by overwatering
or having the ground cake is easily solved by ·

**backfilling over the seed with vermiculite that will
stay moist and open with minimal watering. Do not
fill the planting furrow right up to the top with vermiculite; this will bury the seed far too deeply. Cover
it lightly as before, and fill the furrow in slowly as
the germinating plants take hold and start to grow.**

This, incidentally, is the moment in which the **big plastic
barrels** that I keep at the four corners of the plot cease to be
used as trash containers but turn instead into water barrels,
with the lids firmly clamped in place. We live in a community
that always has severe water restrictions imposed upon it in
hot, dry weather; watering is allowed by hose only at nongar-
dening hours or at very limited times of day. We do have a
well, but it is a long way from the vegetable plot, and the water
that comes from it is far too cold for tiny seedlings. Instead I
keep the plastic barrels regularly filled with water, either from
the well or from the hose. Sometimes I fill the barrels at night
in the company of the cat and ten thousand mosquitoes that

long to lay their eggs in the water—hence the emphasis on keeping the lid on the barrel! The water in the barrels heats up in the hot sun, and I must take care that I don't pour boiling water on my plants, but other than this slight danger they form a wonderful reservoir into which I dip watering cans and carry water in carefully controlled quantities where it is most needed, which is usually around the germinating seedlings of all the second plantings. Four 30-gallon-size plastic cans hold an immense amount of water: enough for gardeners who do not mulch to provide much-needed water for tomatoes, melons, squash, and cucumbers, all of which suffer in unmulched ground in a prolonged drought.

I no longer wait until an entire row of a first crop has been harvested to **refurbish the land and plant more seed.** Instead I now concentrate on harvesting one section of a row of early seeded plants rather than choosing the largest plants from the whole length of the row, and as soon as 2 or 3 feet of space become available, I go into action. I replant New Zealand spinach, for example (of which a very little goes a long way), in the first part of a row that is still occupied by either beets or carrots. Oak-leaf lettuce, which does reasonably well in hot weather, goes into the next section of the row that opens up, and bush beans into the third. As I harvest the early crops of bush beans, peas, or spinach, I replant these with carrots, beets, and turnips. When I grow corn I make consecutive plantings of corn (you can also plant varieties with different maturity dates) in the area reserved for that crop alone. In this case I pull off the mulch and plant a new block of corn, without adding fertilizer, a process that has to end with us around the middle of July. When the weather begins to cool off in mid-August, I set out a row of fall preraised broccoli that has been started elsewhere in the yard (page 121), and I sow spinach where the summer onions have been harvested.

Harvesting a short row of any one crop intensively, and immediately rejuvenating and replanting that area, has provided us with a much more continuous harvest than my old method, in which I replanted a

whole row only after every previous plant in that row had been harvested.

New gardeners will feel better repaid for the work a vegetable plot demands if there is always something available for eating. And if the reseeding fails, try again. There's nothing lost by trying if you have seed left over.

Early Summer Seeding for Fall Harvest

Broccoli   Cabbage   Cauliflower

Hardy Plants for Late Summer Seeding

Beets	Kale	Spinach
Carrots	Leeks	Parsnips
Chard	Lettuce	Turnips
Collards	Mustard	

I have never had the slightest success trying to grow **fall peas,** and **fall spinach** is also not nearly as easy as is sometimes suggested. If spinach is sown very early, as soon as the ground is workable, it may be possible to harvest two crops, providing a succession sowing is made as soon as the first crop is well above ground. For a fall crop seeding must wait until the nights and the ground have slightly cooled off (around mid-September for us). Sowing at that time may produce a successful late fall crop, if the plant resists a variety of diseases. But if you are mad about spinach greens I would suggest that novice gardeners rely on the so-called New Zealand spinach, which will carry on until the first frost, rather than burden themselves with trying to raise a late crop of finicky true spinach.

How late to keep on with succession planting depends upon the average date of the first killing frost in your area and

the plants you are sowing. Killing frost is one that shrivels all but the most hardy foliage but does not freeze the ground. Our first killing frost normally comes late in October. By using varieties of vegetables with a short growing season, which is exactly what I also use when I sow seed in the spring, I continue to sow seed of beans, beets, and carrots up to the end of the first week of August, and I usually gather a good crop. One year, according to my records, when rabbits took an unprecedented delight in our **chard,** I reseeded a row (after indignantly fencing the plot) around the 15th of August. We harvested small but delicious leaves from this row until early November, since chard is extremely cold-tolerant. Such a late sowing would not have been possible with bush beans, which are frost tender.

These liberties cannot, however, be taken with any of the **cabbage family** that are wanted for fall eating. Though all members of the clan are very cold-tolerant when they are fully grown, they need time to develop. Little plants of broccoli, for example, have to be started as early as late June to be ready for harvesting in the fall. As small seedlings the brassicas do not mind hot weather, but they will not change gears, as it were, and move into the stage where they become edible until after the nights have begun to cool off. In June, some gardeners sow a row of whichever fall brassica they use in their main plot, and either thin these out or move them into another growing space as room opens up. I have found that the ravages of the cabbage and other leaf-eating worms wreak havoc on this direct seeding, so I raise my fall crops as I do spring seedlings (for that process see pages 135 ff.) except that I do not have to "harden them off." As a result I've had excellent plants ready to set outside exactly when I want them.

When the weather forecasts predict the **first frost,** tender crops can often be protected by sheets of newspaper, sheets of plastic, or old burlap bags. The first frosts usually are light, and though there can be several of them, they are often followed by a long spell of fine, frost-free weather. For that reason it is well worth trying to save some tender crops, such as bush and pole beans, cucumbers, lettuce, and squash, that do not ripen

well indoors. I have my doubts about trying to save tomatoes, since these will ripen easily indoors.

Don't bother to protect root crops; a touch of frost makes them sweeter

and they will self-store perfectly happily in the ground until you have to clear them out in order to do the fall soil preparation.

Broccoli, cabbage, Swiss chard, kale, and spinach do not need protection against early frost.

After mid-August areas of the ground that become vacant either should be kept steadily weeded or should be covered thickly with mulch. It may be too late to sow vegetables for harvesting, but it is far from being too late for weed seeds to get themselves strongly entrenched!

Once the long-lasting kale crops have been harvested and really hard, freezing weather seems just around the corner (for us usually in early November) **clean all the seasonal debris off the ground and take it to the compost pile.** Do not put the debris that comes off a vegetable plot through a shredder and spread it straight back onto the land, as plant diseases and plant pests winter over in dead plant material even when it is shredded. It takes the internal heat of a compost pile to kill problems that exist in dead plants. I cut my perennial herbs growing in my vegetable plot, to the ground, but it is not absolutely necessary to do so. Parsley is a biennial and sometimes comes through a fairly mild winter; in its second year parsley is, however, absolutely determined to go to seed. Nothing can stop it, and it ceases to produce edible leaves. I leave our parsley to the very last moment, working over every other part of the plot except the place where it is growing. But in the end I do pull it out every year, for I have never found parsley to be very satisfactory in its second season. If you let it go to seed, it will reseed itself and provide you with an automatic succession of plants.

After compost is piled onto the plot and raked roughly, the ground can be covered with grass clippings, if they are still

available, or fallen leaves for a winter mulch. These do not carry plant pests.

If you do not mulch, have the ground go into winter as free of weeds as is humanly possible.

Many weeds are, unfortunately, perennial. If you do not clean them off in the fall, they will reappear as giants refreshed and hinder your effort at spring planting. If you have grown your garden blind the first year with no idea of its pH or nutritional values, this is also the time to have it tested or to test it yourself in the manner described earlier (pages 33–35).

Cucumbers

Container Growing

Some vegetables can be successfully grown like oversize pot plants in large individual containers, deep planting boxes, plastic tubs, or even specially built wooden trays, which must have a depth of anything from 6 to 10 inches but can be whatever length and width the grower has space to provide. This is an excellent way to add an extra growing area to a small yard, to find the ideal conditions for sun-loving plants, or to indulge in a little fire escape or rooftop gardening. A patio that is extremely sunny will not only provide the necessary hours of sunlight but will also supply certain plants, eggplant, for example, with reflected heat, something that is a great help in getting a good crop in areas with a short growing season.

My principal vegetable plot is situated beside the terrace of a house that has been pulled down. This old terrace is both very sunny and very sheltered and has, therefore, proved an invaluable adjunct to the main plot as a place to grow vegetables in containers. Watering is simple there, and the tubs and the plot get their vital daily inspection at the same time. But though this heat-reflecting terrace is a convenience, it is not a necessity.

Container vegetables can be grown anywhere where there is a full day of sunlight, shelter from the wind, and water readily accessible.

It's the rare house that doesn't have some sunny position, if it's only on the front doorsteps, and tomatoes or cucumbers neatly trained in tubs beside the front doorstep are, at the very least, a fine conversation piece!

The **containers** themselves vary with the depth of the grower's purse and their need for elegance. All types of commercial individual containers are readily available, most of them rather expensive. They include large terra cotta imported pots, sometimes glazed, lightweight cement pots, deep and very heavy stone planters, redwood tubs and boxes, and ornamental tubs made from an enormous range of plastic materials. I have no quarrel with any of them, just as long as they have adequate drainage holes at the bottom, which, unfortunately, is not always the case.

Vegetables growing in containers have to be compensated for their unnatural life style by extra fertilizer, very porous soil, and copious water. And they will not do well unless surplus water can drain out very fast; this means that the **drainage holes** must be more than just adequate. Drainage holes can often be added or made larger by the buyer of a commercial product, but not always, and not without danger of breaking the expensive purchase. This is something to check very carefully.

There is, however, no need to confine growing vegetables in containers to elegant and costly pieces of equipment. I have had great success with plants in circular or square plastic wastepaper baskets that are 15 inches in diameter, taper to around 10 inches at the base, and have a depth of 18 inches. I've also grown excellent vegetables in 5-gallon plastic tubs, in the plastic buckets sold as diaper containers, and in small 11-quart plastic buckets. With **plastic containers** the drainage vents should be made around the very lowest level of the sides of the container; two holes, one immediately above the other, about 3 inches apart in a ring around the entire container will do the trick. Do not bore holes in the bottom of any plastic container; so many are needed for proper drainage that the base may be too much weakened to be able to hold the weight of the soil. Those very lightweight should, in theory, be much

more liable to get knocked over by heavy winds than those made of more solid materials. This may well be true if staked tomatoes or tall pole beans, which would offer considerable wind resistance, are grown in them, but these I have never grown in tubs. I grow early tomatoes, which I allow to sprawl so there is no wind resistance, and I have not had a problem of a plastic tub tipping over.

If growers can lay their hands on what are rapidly becoming obsolete, nostalgic objects, old **wine cases** or **apple boxes,** or even **bushel baskets,** all make excellent containers for vegetables. Bushel baskets can be lined with plastic, in which a great many holes should be punched, both at the bottom and around the sides. There are also large, round plastic clothes baskets which, with a lining, could serve as a long-lasting container. Wooden boxes need to be treated on the inside with a nontoxic wood preservative and can be painted on the outside in any color that suits the grower's taste. Home handymen can, of course, easily make deep, elegant wooden boxes or shallow planting trays, any size that they want, out of redwood or whatever lumber is available. Rough-sawn lumber, one inch thick, does better than finished lumber for planters. Make a single row of drainage vents around the outer edge of wooden containers and at least two circular rows on the base of the box, and a big hole in the very center.

I burn **drainage holes** with a red-hot screwdriver in plastic containers, and I have sometimes burned holes in wooden boxes. Admittedly this has led to an occasional flickering flame, so a bit and brace is probably the wiser way to make the holes. With metal containers I punch out the holes with a mallet and an old screwdriver. Any container that has drainage holes in the base should always be raised off the ground to allow surplus water to drain out even faster. I raise my wooden containers on bricks, largely because I seem to have an unending supply of old bricks tucked away at the back of the house, but neat wooden cleats nailed to the bottom of a box or a big planting tray are just as satisfactory, as long as there is good clearance between the bottom of the box and the ground itself. There are innumerable books, particularly the admirable Sun-

set series, that provide step-by-step instructions for making planting boxes of every sort.

An excellent way to grow plants in containers is to use **construction material that is open-ended** and stands directly on the ground rather than on a terrace. This does away with the need for drainage holes, raising the containers, and so on. It is worth digging up the ground on which the ring or block, whatever it is to be, is to stand, so that the plant roots can drive even more deeply down if they wish. I have had wonderful results using open-ended rings that were the couplings for large water pipes; they are made of asbestos and are about 2 feet in diameter. But I have come across these only once by chance, and have not been able to lay my hands on more. I mention their existence in case an inquiry to your local water department might turn up some. Outlets that sell building supplies, particularly cement products used for house construction, offer what are known as "**chimney blocks,**" open-ended cement squares designed to fit around a tile chimney flue. They are sold as individual units, 8 by 8 inches or 8 by 13 inches, an excellent size for container growing, and are very inexpensive.

To my mind, container boxes or planters are nothing but oversized flower pots. In spite of what I increasingly see suggested in various publications, I still think it is better to provide **internal drainage** inside any freestanding containers. The modern reasoning is that so long as soil does not block the drainage holes, which can be prevented with fine mesh screening, there is no need to take up space with an internal dry well of coarse gravel or shards. If there were only one or two drainage holes per container, I would be perfectly willing to accept this reasoning. But since multiple drainage holes up the sides as well as in the base make a huge difference to the success of container plants, I still feel that a dry well or drainage layer is absolutely essential. For this, peastone gravel is excellent, and, as an added bonus, its weight will anchor the plastic tubs more firmly. With most containers this drainage material should cover the entire base to a depth of at least half an inch. In plastic containers, in which there's always a greater danger that

the soil may become and stay too wet because there is no evaporation through the plastic sides, there should be enough drainage material to rise above the level of the upper holes along the sides of the container. Do not use sand for this drainage pad. Sand packs down and holds surplus moisture, rather than allowing it to pass through.

The trick with container cultivation is to use a rich, porous mixture as a **growing medium,** which will hold water long enough to be useful to the roots but never stay too wet or dry out too fast. This is not easy to manage.

> **For my containers I make a mixture of two parts finished compost and one part soil dug up from a growing area, with builders' sand added in sufficient quantity to give the mixture a gritty feeling.**

I use sand because it's less expensive than perlite, and it stays in place in the mixture. Perlite has an unfortunate habit in container growing of slowly washing up to the top of the soil surface. If you have no space for a pile of sand in the yard, perlite will do the job. Since I know the pH of my compost, I do not test the mixture. For those who use peat moss in place of compost, a test might be important; peat moss is acid, and vegetables do not enjoy very high acidity. The test, therefore, would be to see whether a handful or two of agricultural limestone might not be needed with every wheelbarrow load of the soil mixture.

Another of the problems of container vegetable growing is getting the roots enough nutrients, and there are all kinds of ways that this can be managed.

> **One is to add 5-10-5 fertilizer to the potting soil at the rate of a tablespoon and a half to every 10-quart plastic bucketful of soil. This should be put in the lower level of the container; the 2 upper inches of soil mix should not contain fertilizer. Another method of making sure the plants get enough nourishment is to add liquid fertilizer every second week after it is obvious that the plants are really growing well.**

I vary the liquid concentrates that I use; sometimes I use organic fish emulsion, other times I use chemical water-soluble fertilizers that I slosh over the foliage of the plant as well as pour into the soil. It has been my experience that plants do better with a change of diet where fertilizers are concerned. I cannot offer any safe and easy rule for the proper addition of fertilizer, for the amount a plant in a container needs depends on the speed with which it is growing, the basic richness of the soil mix around its roots, and, above all, the weather. Growers must use their own judgment: if the foliage appears to be growing very fast and rather too lushly and to look very dark in color, then reduce by half the amount of fertilizer you have been giving and give it much less thereafter. In containers in which 5-10-5 has been mixed into the basic soil it is most unlikely that extra fertilizer of any kind will be needed until the plants start to crop quite heavily.

Since it takes an experienced hand and eye to decide when and if container plants need extra nutrients, beginning gardeners might be wise to use instead some of the **slow or controlled-release fertilizers,** which have a high phosphorus count. This material is incorporated into the soil mix before it goes into the container, just like the 5-10-5, but very little of it is needed, and the specifications given on the bag must be followed exactly. The advantage of the slow-release fertilizer is that it dissolves extremely slowly, giving off nutrients only as these become deficient in the soil. It does away with any additional fertilizing during the growing season and, used as directed, eliminates the danger of overfertilizing. The high phosphorus count that it contains is a great stimulus to excellent crop production. Controlled or slow-release fertilizers exist in many forms, often with the word *urea* in front of them. Not all of them are balanced fertilizers—that is to say, not all of them have the necessary trace elements in them—so study the labels carefully before you make your purchase.

Vegetables can also be grown in pots and containers in **soilless mixes,** and this is extremely useful for people who want to grow a few salad pickings in a window box or want to garden on a roof where weight is a matter of concern. I have

For Container Growing

Bunching onions   Herbs
Bush zucchini   Lettuce
Cucumbers   Peppers
Determinate tomatoes   Vining squash
Eggplant

had no personal experience with this method of growing vegetables, but I understand that the packaged synthetic mixes of
equal quantities of damp peat moss and vermiculite with the
addition of a tablespoon of limestone and a slow-release high-
phosphorus fertilizer to each pailful of mix form a very fine
growing medium. This would, however, be an expensive way
to handle a large number of container plants, for the mix is not
cheap and a great deal will be needed. Soilless mixes can also
be used without incorporating slow-release fertilizer but with
minute amounts of chemical fertilizer regularly added to the
watering can. But if this second method is used, the soil must
be thoroughly flushed through with plain water every third
week to avoid a dangerous buildup of mineral salts, which will
harm the plant roots, a problem which goes hand in hand with
fertilizing every time the watering can is applied.

The main danger with all container-grown vegetables occurs at the **very earliest stage:** when their roots are much too
small to keep the large amount of soil or mix in the container
properly aerated. If the mix or soil becomes soaking wet at this
point, root rot can easily set in. In extremely wet weather while
the container plants are still tiny, I put stakes into the soil and
throw a sheet of plastic over the top with the ends falling

outside the container to drain off the rain. Once the plants have started strong growth the problem reverses itself; then the most important part of container growing is to make sure that the soil or medium never dries out and that the plants are constantly surrounded with a pleasantly moist mixture. To this end I **mulch** the soil surface of my containers. For those in a very prominent position, I use bark mulch or buckwheat hulls, of which, happily, I still have a large supply, though I'm not sure that they are any longer obtainable commercially. For those on the old terrace beside the vegetable garden I use grass clippings, just as I do in the plot itself. With soilless mixes the mulch ought to be an inorganic material, and a layer of coarse gravel spread thickly on top of a soilless mix forms an excellent barrier to the evaporation of moisture.

Regular watering is absolutely essential to container gardening, and it's equally important to make sure when you water that enough is given for surplus water always to drain out. A little dribble of water will do far more harm than good.

With all containers, always feel the soil at least an inch below the surface. Get your hand underneath the mulch and poke your finger right in before rewatering. This is the only way to avoid having the soil become sodden and driving out the air, which, in turn, does lasting damage to the root system.

My experience with this kind of growing is obviously very limited compared with those high-rise gardeners who raise an astonishing variety of vegetables in this manner. For the most part I use 5-gallon plastic containers, and in these I have grown with great success cucumbers and determinate tomatoes, both of which I allow to hang down over the sides of the containers and spread slowly over the heat-reflecting stone terrace, thus ripening the crops very well and very early. I have also raised bush zucchini, eggplant, and peppers successfully this way. Container plants will do better if they are not crowded. Lack of **air circulation** is a great problem if several are put into a rather small pot. This is, of course, a matter of the amount of space available. Five-gallon tubs will usually hold two plants

fairly well, but three will produce serious overcrowding and almost instant pest problems.

When the growing season is over I pull out the plants and dump the contents of the containers onto the compost pile. If the vegetables were raised in a soilless mix this can be stored over the winter in plastic bags. The reason for emptying the containers is to make sure they can be thoroughly washed and cleaned up before the next growing season. A dirty container presents potential soil and pest problems. If the containers have to be left outside over the winter for lack of storage space, turn them upside down so there is no chance of ice and snow getting in and cracking them.

I also use containers to raise the few culinary **herbs** that our household enjoys, but these I plant either in flue tiles or in 6- or 8-inch pots.

> **Herbs, with a few exceptions, have the strongest flavor if they're grown in rather lean, sweet soil, so I use mainly garden soil with very little compost added,**

and since I know our soil to be acid, I thoroughly pepper my mix with ground limestone, mixed in well. Those who buy their soil should get the type known as Sandy Soil Mix and add a third by volume of damp sphagnum or damp peat moss, together once more with a heavy peppering of ground limestone. Potted herbs do best in full sun with plenty of air circulation, so do not crowd the pots close to each other for effect. They need no fertilizer in the soil or added to the container during the growing season. They will need regular watering. Their requirement for superfast drainage is even more acute than for the other container-grown vegetables, and for that reason I am again strongly in favor of adding crocking material to the base of the container in which they are grown.

Sweet marjoram, basil, chives, parsley, summer savory, rosemary, and the various thymes all do well for me in pots. Mints, which need less sun and a richer soil, I grow in containers mainly in compost on the shady side of the terrace. New gardeners should buy prestarted herbs. Herbs can be started

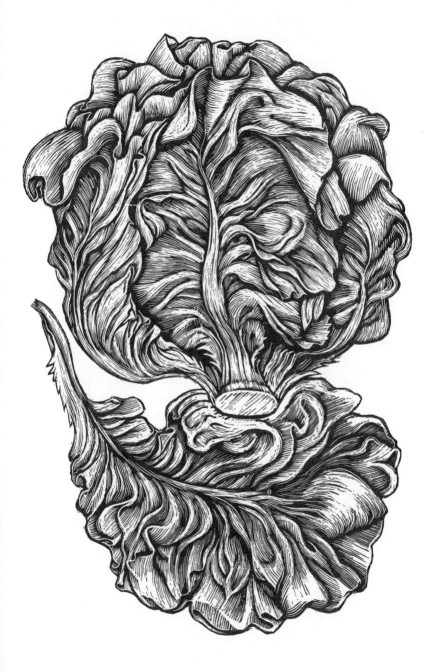

Lettuce

from seeds indoors, just like any other vegetables, but starting seeds indoors is not something I recommend for novice gardeners. In many cases the perennial herbs will have to be brought indoors in the winter if they are to survive safely in their pots. Generally speaking, potted herbs that have been grown in containers outdoors all summer can be brought indoors to a windowsill in the winter, but a readjustment period should be expected. In late August you can also take cuttings of these plants and start new specimens for indoor gardening.

In spite of the fact that I have grown excellent herbs in pots on the terrace, I frankly prefer to grow my herbs along the edges of the vegetable plot. It would be a very small garden that could not accommodate the number of herbs that the average gardener uses in the kitchen. It is possible that the rich soil of the garden may diminish their aromatic content to a limited degree, but not enough to make me give up this trouble-free method of growing them alongside the other vegetables, as against day-by-day attention needed by herbs in pots. But for those who have no sunny spot, do not allow yourself to be intimidated by all the lore and mystique that surrounds herbs and their culture. An herb is nothing but a plant with rather specific cultural problems that are not very hard to meet. If you can manage to bring potted geraniums to full bloom in a sunny space, you can manage to grow potted herbs; this, I think, is a word of comfort that many new gardeners would do well to remember.

Starting Plants Indoors

 Sooner or later most indoor gardeners are overwhelmed with a desire to sow indoors the vegetables that need a long growing season and must be set into the ground as well-started plants if they are to bring a good harvest. This is a fine idea, as it is the only way you can be sure of getting the exact varieties you want. But, on the whole, I think it advisable to have a year, preferably more, of vegetable gardening behind you, and to have developed the sort of "feel" for it that can come only from experience, before you undertake this finicky side of home horticulture.

While it is possible to raise plants indoors from seed with nothing more than a sunny windowsill for growing space, to grow really sturdy plants you need to be able to provide them with three different environments at various stages of their development: a warm, dark place for germination; or a fluorescent light unit or a cool, sunny place for growing on once they have passed the emerging seedling stage; and a cold but controlled and protected place where they can be "hardened" or gradually accustomed to life outdoors.

Timing is also crucial. Plants must not go outdoors immature, nor can they wait around a long time in the house getting weaker and weaker because they were started too early. To help you plan your starting times, you will need to collect

information on how long each plant will need for germination, leaf development, and growth, for these differ from plant to plant. Sometimes this information is printed on the seed packet, and you need only apply it to local weather conditions. If it is not on the packet, you can usually get such information from the seed company on request.

In areas where there is winter frost, January is the best time to start assembling seeds, information, and equipment for this kind of home horticulture. Once the seeds are in hand, make a second planning chart (assuming that you have already made a planting plan for the actual plot) which indicates when you must begin the germination process for your various vegetables, both the ones you will start indoors and those that will be sown directly in the garden. The information on the seed packets is extremely important and should be carefully studied in advance.

The **containers for starting seeds** can be purchased from seed companies or from garden centers, or they can be made from all kinds of recycled kitchen and food equipment. Aluminum containers in which frozen food is packaged make excellent seed flats, so long as holes are punched in the bottom for drainage. The cut-down bases of quart or even half-gallon milk cartons, again with special drainage holes, also serve very well, as do cottage cheese cartons, plastic margarine boxes, and even the thoroughly washed-out, cut-down bases of large Clorox bottles. I have found that square containers are much simpler to use than anything that is circular, and that goes for the pots used for the later planting up. This has nothing to do with the growing process; a seedling will sprout just as easily in a round container as it will in a square one. I prefer square receptacles and square plastic pots for the later stages because they can be packed close together into less space than round containers or pots.

The best **growing mediums** for seed sprouting are the synthetic soil mixes, all of which can be bought at garden stores, specially packaged for seed sowing. It is also possible to make your own soilless mix from sieved sphagnum, perlite, and vermiculite, but this seems to me an unnecessary complication, since seed germinates equally well in plain vermicu-

Start Indoors

Broccoli

Cabbage

Cauliflower

Celery

Eggplant

Head Lettuce

Peppers

Tomatoes

lite if you don't want to use the mixtures put up by the stores. I have always found that a pad of damp, well-wrung-out, long-fiber sphagnum moss, which can also be bought in small bags at any garden center, put into the bottom of the container in which the seed is to be planted, stimulates root growth. Even more importantly, it acts as a moisture reservoir that will prevent the synthetic soil mix that surrounds the seed from fatal drying out, a problem to which sieved sphagnum or synthetic mixes are dangerously prone. If this happens even once during the process of germination all the seedlings will die.

If you have laid in a winter supply of **soil,** it too can be used for seed sprouting, providing you first rub it through a fine mesh screen to eliminate all roughage. Soil does, however, contain not only weed seed, but also the fungus of various diseases, a problem that causes a disaster known as "damping off." This is an incurable condition that will topple a row of healthy seedlings overnight, just as you are beginning to gloat over their fine appearance. One way to rid the soil of all these organisms is to heat it (160 degrees for an hour, making certain that all of the soil reaches that temperature for the specified time) in small batches in the kitchen oven—a process that, in these days of energy conservation, is really not worth the effort. You can also drench the soil with a product, such as Damp-Off, made specifically for this problem, or with boiling water.

If you're anxious to use **individual pots** from the start to

avoid root disturbance, seed can be sown in paper cups with drainage holes punched in the base, in commercially purchased small (2¼-inch) square peat pots, in special individual compressed peat cubes, or in compressed peat pellets. If you choose to work with peat pellets, be sure to purchase the ones which are not enclosed in plastic netting and are, therefore, completely biodegradable (see pages 105–6). You can also buy specially sectioned plastic, Tufflite, or six-pack plant containers. Peat pots, whether you buy the square kind or the round type, or little blocks of compressed peat need to stand in containers; again, discarded aluminum food trays or cut-down milk cartons will do very well.

All peat pots should stand far enough apart so that damp vermiculite can surround them on all sides; I have found this to be the only way of making sure that the walls of peat pots do not get so hard that the roots cannot penetrate them. The expanded peat pellets, on the other hand, have a tendency to remain much too wet, and for this reason should stand free in a container so that air can circulate around them.

Anything in which seed is being grown must have drainage holes at the base, so every container needs to be stood on a tray or on something into which the surplus water can drain. Stores where you buy commercial peat pots will also sell special trays that can hold them. These trays should contain either aggregate, sand, perlite, or vermiculite—anything to provide a dry well into which surplus water will run and from which it will in turn evaporate to provide humidity for the seedlings. If you don't want to buy a special container, an old tray will do the job, though very often it is sensible to line it with heavy plastic in order to prevent rust. Some of the containers treated with waterproof acrylic polymer sprays available at hardware stores will do the same job. The waterproof boxes sold for kitty litter and the clay-type kitty litter itself also form perfectly good evaporation trays on which to set potted seedlings.

The **seeding process** in itself is not hard. If you're using containers, pour in the growing medium or soil substitute,

which you have premoistened, to within a half inch of the top and firm it down, particularly along the edges of a square container. It is advisable to premoisten or dampen the soil substitute in a separate container. Never forget that seeds need to be sown on an even, firm surface.

Sow the seed about half an inch apart, cover very lightly with more of the moist medium, and press that down, too. Slip the containers or pots into plastic bags, but don't let the bag rest on the growing medium. You can also cover the containers with a sheet of glass. Most seeds prefer to germinate in the dark, so move the containers into a dark, warm place.

It will also be necessary to provide some means of getting **bottom heat** under the containers, for most tender plants need more than house heat in order to trigger the germination process. Commercial water-resistant heating cables are available in various wattages and lengths, and these can be spread around, with perfect safety, in the medium onto which the seed containers drain. For years I used a forty-watt electric light bulb on a trouble-light fixture for heat. For safety's sake the lamp was laid on an old metal car license plate inside a wooden wine box. This made a heat chamber through which the warmth slowly radiated into the tray above and brought me excellent germination.

A warm cupboard near the stove is also excellent. If your refrigerator gives off a little heat, standing the bags on the top of that will do the trick with a tent of newspaper over them to provide the needed darkness. If you're using heating cables, I have found it better to cover the seed containers with glass rather than with plastic bags or Saran Wrap. For one thing it is a great deal easier to lay newspaper over glass, but the principal reason is not as simple as that. Seeds sealed into plastic bags and set onto heating cables become enveloped in a tremendously moist atmosphere, and the recycled moisture pours down the sides of the bags, keeping the soil almost too wet. This often rots the seed and, worse still, will cause mildew on the seedlings as they emerge. With glass over the container

this problem can be handled by reversing the glass and wiping off the wet condensation. One can, of course, turn the plastic bag inside out, and that is indeed essential for plants that take a long time to germinate, eggplant for example. As soon as any growth appears remove all forms of covering from the containers, and get them into strong light to avoid excessively leggy stems.

When seed is sown in individual containers, two or three seeds in each are all that is necessary.

When compressed peat cubes or pellets that expand with water are used, allow these to drain for at least twenty-four hours in the open air in a warm room before the seed is sown.

Without this precaution the interior of the pellet often remains far too wet for successful germination. Seeds can be planted in peat cubes or pellets by making a small hole with a pencil point for each individual seed.

When the first true leaves (the first pair of leaves are "seedling leaves" and bear no resemblance to the true leaves) of the plant have formed, those that are growing in unsectioned flats should be transferred into 3- or 4-inch peat pots or recycled cut-down milk cartons or paper cups with punched-out drainage holes. Again use one of the synthetic mixes as a soil substitute. The roots of plants grown in the synthetic mix or in vermiculite will come very easily out of the soil and will be extremely lavish. It is, however, wise to water the flat or container about an hour before transplanting in order to be sure that the seedlings are turgid (full of water) and can take the shock of being moved.

Whether in flats or individual containers, the special, commercially prepared soil substitutes used contain mild additions of important nutrients, which will enable the plants to develop properly even though the basic ingredients in which they are growing are sterile. If you are using vermiculite by itself as the growing medium, remember that this contains no nutritious properties at all, so the seedlings must be fed a very weak solution of a balanced, chemical, water-soluble fertilizer, such

as Hyponex or Rapid-Gro, every other time they are watered. Chemical fertilizer is used because, unlike organic fertilizer, it does not depend on soil bacteria to start it working and to break down the nutrients in it. Synthetic soil contains no soil bacteria, so an organic fertilizer, such as fish emulsion, will only form useless slime in and on the growing medium of which the roots can make no use.

Light will be extremely important for the seedlings as they emerge. A house windowsill, no matter how sunny, will not provide sufficient light unless the pots or containers are rotated daily. Part of this problem can be met by smoothing aluminum foil over large sheets of cardboard and using these as reflectors propped up behind the seedling plants. This doubles the amount of light that they will get from a sunny window and cuts down on their tendency to lean toward the sun, which is very bad for their subsequent long-term health.

In my opinion, by far the best and most worthwhile purchase anyone who intends to grow seedlings indoors can make is an **artificial light unit** with fluorescent tubes and a tray that fits underneath it. These units can be purchased at horticultural

Two-tube fluorescent light unit

centers and from some seed companies, such as Park Seed. Artificial light units do not make all that much difference in the actual germination of the seed, but they are a tremendous help to the little plants once germination has taken place and can be used even during the germination process. With artificial lights that are adjusted so that they are constantly 5 inches above the growing tips of the plants and set on a timer that will automatically provide fourteen hours of artificial sunlight, plants can be grown in a cool place indoors and remain stocky and strong and healthy in a way that is almost impossible for those that are being raised on a windowsill. In general, if the leaves of the plants droop, increase the distance from the lights; if they reach upward, decrease the distance.

The plants should be reduced to the single largest seedling as soon as the true leaves appear, by cutting out the extras at ground level. Do not pull them out, for this produces root disturbance that will seriously affect the remaining plant. As the plants develop, move them into larger pots.

This is particularly important for tomatoes, eggplants, and peppers, all of which need a long period indoors before they can be safely planted out. And since this time amounts, in many areas, to almost two months, it is of great importance to repot the plant as the roots fill the container, in order that there should be no disruption in the growth. When seedlings are replanted they should be set more deeply into the growing medium in the new container than they were in the old.

The first move with plants in peat pots or peat pellets should come when the roots appear through the sides of their growing container. Rich compost can be used for the additional soil in the new pot, but if you have no compost, buy some sterile soil from a garden shop. The reason for using compost at this stage is to get the plants used to finding their nourishment in a nonsynthetic medium. This makes their transfer to ground growing much easier when that time comes. The first move is usually into a 3-inch to 4-inch square pot. If the plant outgrows this while the weather is still cool, shift it into a

6-inch pot. With tomatoes, at every shift always bury the plant up to the first set of leaves to take advantage of the root-making capacity of tomato stems.

Remember the aim at all times is to keep the plants in active growth with no disruption in root growth but with short, stocky top growth. And to get that short, stocky, pest-free top growth you will need cool growing conditions (not over 60 degrees at night) and the maximum possible light (sunlight for at least half the day and bright light for the rest of the day).

But no matter whether the plants are grown in a window or under artificial lights they cannot be planted outdoors without undergoing a process known as "**hardening off.**" What this amounts to is conditioning the plants to lower temperature by day and by night to less and less water, and the only way this can be properly accomplished is by working in rather slow stages.

The first step in hardening plants is to **reduce the water they receive**—though not of course to such a degree that the plants start to wilt. While this is going on, prepare a cold frame to accommodate the very hardy plants that will be the first to be put into the garden. I read accounts of people conditioning their plants by setting them onto a child's wagon and trundling them outside for an increasing number of hours each day for about a week. This seems to me to be yet another example of heroic self-sacrifice on the part of the grower and not particularly satisfactory, since the weather can change suddenly while the plants are outside and kill or stunt their growth. I do not think that home-grown plants can be successfully hardened off without a **cold frame.** This is a piece of equipment that vegetable gardeners who insist upon raising their own plants would be well advised to own.

A plant frame of any type is basically an open-bottomed box with the back higher than the front. The back should be about 15 inches high and the front about 9 inches. The box is laid on the ground facing due south and the exposed sides backed with soil thrown against them to prevent drafts from

Cold Frame

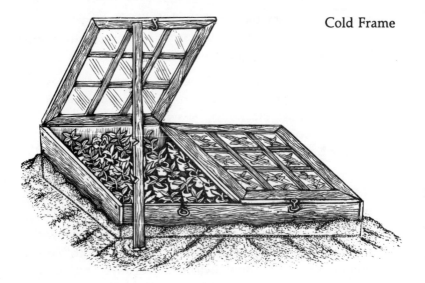

creeping in underneath and to add extra overall insulation. There must also be a tightly fitting top. Tightly fitting tops can be made from old storm windows with a base of the box tailored exactly to fit these dimensions, or from scrap lumber held together with angle irons and with heavy plastic stapled to it. In areas where spring sometimes brings heavy snow the cover is best made of glass. In other climates heavy plastic covers are perfectly acceptable. The back of the top should be hinged with ordinary door hinges to the back of the box frame. The front of the frame should have a hook and the top should have an eye, so that the wind cannot blow a lightweight top up or off. The lightweight prefabricated aluminum cold frame, which costs between forty and sixty dollars, serves very adequately in areas where early spring weather is unlikely to fall below zero except under freak conditions. In colder regions it might be wiser to have the framework constructed from 2-by-6 boarding, and for long life these boards, of course, should be treated with any wood preservative that does not contain creosote.

By the time the sun is heating up in spring, the temperature

inside a cold frame that faces south and is protected at the back, or on the north side, by a fence, wall, or a thick row of bushes, can rise to over 70 degrees very quickly. This can be easily watched with an ordinary thermometer, but for the best results I would suggest the worthwhile investment in a maximum-minimum thermometer, which, as long as you remember to reset it every day, will tell you how high the temperature went by day and how low by night. The temperature for plants set into a cold frame should not be above 70 degrees by day; this you avoid by propping open the lid of the frame. When the plants first go out, the frames should be closed in the early afternoon while the sun is still shining on them. This will build up sufficient heat inside to keep the frame warm even if there is light frost. Plants coming from indoors are sensitive to bright sunlight. They are best set out on a cloudy day, or if the weather is sunny, newspaper should be thrown over the top of the frame. If the weather turns unusually cold then extra heat can be retained by throwing an old quilt over the top.

The trick to conditioning the plants you have in the frame is to open the cover for longer and longer intervals until it is possible to leave it open by day and by night without the plants suffering.

When this stage is reached the plants are ready to go into the garden.

The only way to decide when to start setting the plants outside is by a combination of common sense (according to the kind of early spring you're having) and the date that you know from the seed package that the plants are usually ready to go into the ground. All members of the cabbage family, for example, are what is known as "cold-hardy." Properly conditioned, they can go into the ground as soon as it is workable; they will not mind light frost just as long as they have been prepared by a slow transference from the heat of the house to the varying temperatures outdoors. The tender plants that are much more susceptible to frost injury take longer to get to the right stage indoors and, therefore, will not be ready to go out into the frame until the danger of frost is much less acute. But, even so,

they should be hardened in frames because a properly placed, properly insulated cold frame will keep out light spring frosts, and even tender plants will not be damaged in it.

This may all sound like rather tricky work, and it does take some learning. It is not something that can really be explained on paper, but rather something the gardener gradually discovers how to manage. I should warn you, however, that if you are growing your own plants and are hardening them off in a cold frame, your presence will be needed not only every single day but during the day. Spring everywhere is a variable, fickle time of year. Sudden cold winds can spring up, and the frame must be closed. It is no good assuming after the plants first go out that you can open the frame in early morning and close it when you come home in the evening. This is the way to kill your plants and to send you rushing around at the last moment trying to find some that have been raised by commercial growers. If you cannot be "on duty" all day, prop the frame open about 3 inches, usually enough to safeguard against excessive heat and afternoon chill.

Another way to prestart your tender vegetables is to use a heated frame. This is the old-fashioned "**hot bed**" method, in which the heat used to be provided by fermenting manure, a process now modernized by using specially made heating cables. The basic ingredient is, again, a cold frame. In areas where spring sometimes brings heavy snow the cover is best made of glass. In other climates heavy plastic covers are perfectly acceptable. The back of a heated frame should always be set against something solid, preferably a house wall, for even in these days of extra insulation some heat usually escapes through a house wall, which will, in turn, affect the amount of heat that is trapped inside the frame. If this is not possible a garage wall or even a fence can be used, but there must always be an electric outlet nearby.

When the frame is being set up, a little tunnel should be dug under one side in order to slide the wire that is to run from the electric outlet to the heating cable underneath the frame. A lot of heat is lost if the heating cable lead is draped over the top of the frame, preventing the cover from closing tightly. In

order to conserve heat, which is the main worry with any kind of frame, the exposed sides should also be heavily insulated. If snow falls heavily on the frame, blocking out the light, leave it alone. Snow is an excellent insulator in itself, and light is diffused through it for the plants it is protecting.

Insulating material that can be used on the sides of a heated frame can be all kinds of things. In northern areas where large quantities of wood chips are sometimes available these can be piled up fairly quickly around the sides and in front and held in place with hardware cloth (small-gauge wire mesh) pegged into the soil with long-legged hooks made from wire coat hangers. Sawdust treated in the same way also makes excellent insulation, as does hay. By the seashore marsh hay and seaweed form good insulating material. For gardeners who have access to none of these special products, sand or soil will also do a good job. Do not try to carry this idea to an extreme by sinking the sides of the frame below ground level. This may indeed trap the warmth a little better, but the sunken frame will become a waterlogged pond as the soil thaws out.

I have used as insulating material large-sized, heavyweight garbage bags filled with commercial-grade vermiculite, available at building supply centers. After some trial and error the method that has worked best for me has been to fill the plastic bags less than half full and then drive out the remaining air by rolling up the empty portions before fastening the top with a knot. The bags are then laid on their sides all around the exposed parts of the frame and piled up one on top of the other like lightweight sand bags. They're kept in position by putting the empty portion of the lower bag over the bag above it and tucking the surplus material underneath the upper bag. My frame takes two layers of bags along the outside and one along the front. When the bags are in place, I cover them with a length of black plastic that is tucked in tightly over the top and under the base of the pile of bags. This in turn is held in place with hardware cloth laid over it as precaution against any inadvertent puncturing of the plastic. The hardware cloth is kept close to the plastic by stakes driven very deeply into the ground. This double play of vermiculite and black plastic insu-

lation has proved extremely effective; it neither deteriorates nor washes out.

The heat for the frame is produced by waterproof heating cables that have a built-in, preset thermostat that will produce a soil temperature of 70 degrees. This cable, which comes in varying lengths and at various wattages according to the climate in which you are gardening, can be bought with all the necessary instructions through almost every seed catalog.

This cable is laid in continuous coils on the ground. They can be set close to each other but must not touch or overlap. As a protection against sharp tools, the cable should be covered with hardware cloth. Over this can be piled 6 inches of compost, if seed is to be sown directly into the ground. If the frame is to be used for prestarted plants, the cable can be covered with 3 inches of soil, sand, or vermiculite. Slugs can be a great nuisance in every type of frame—the comforting heat attracts them. The various baits described on page 154 should be strewn on the ground, or the little plants might be devoured.

Heated frames are even more trouble to watch over than cold frames. Even if the soil thermostat shuts off, the accumulated soil heat combined with sun can quickly drive the interior temperatures into the nineties. The frames need to be opened slightly no matter what the weather to keep a good circulation of air going, and they need to be fully opened whenever there is bright sun but no wind. Wind is a great enemy even to plants in a frame. Plenty of water and misting is needed for plants in either cold or heated frames. I keep a filled watering can inside my frame to avoid giving tender roots a cold douche. The earlier the heat cable can be dispensed with in a heated frame the healthier the plants inside it will be. Although a heated frame is a great help to those who garden in very cold climates, since it makes possible the use of a frame long before it could otherwise be used, the heat itself will weaken the plants unless it is very carefully watched. I use my heating cables as a fail-safe auxiliary for abnormally cold snaps rather than as a continuous means of providing heat, for this is the simplest way to handle a useful tool that can get out of hand. Heated frames are also excellent for crops of early lettuce

seeded directly into the soil. They will nurture fall lettuce and radishes after frost has put an end to outdoor vegetable growing. To me their great advantage is the fact that I can get prestarted plants out from under the lights and into a frame far earlier when I know that heat is available, which makes the success rate of indoor seeding much higher.

Radish

Pests and Diseases

I am inclined to take a rather upbeat attitude about the problem of pests and diseases in the vegetable garden. In my experience all the known blights, molds, fungi, and what-have-you are unlikely to strike every plant at once every year and ruin your entire crop. Weather conditions or other factors may bring mildew or other diseases, sometimes, to the home garden, but don't plan an "impregnable" line of defense against them, assuming automatically they will appear. Plant diseases are also much less liable to attack vegetables that are grown in **well-prepared soil,** with plenty of space for **good air circulation** between the rows and around the individual plants, and in **full sun,** with the **proper moisture** regularly available.

Buying disease-resistant plants and seeds and providing healthy growing conditions are at least as important for the prevention of plant disease as are strong poisons.

Diseases that come through the soil are best thwarted by trying to grow vegetables in different parts of the plot, not only in successive plantings the same season, but also in successive years. That is why the planting plan should not be thrown away after the season is over, but filed where it (and those of

the years before) can easily be consulted. If a plot is so small that **plant rotation** every successive season is almost impossible, and this can happen with tiny plots, then large quantities of fresh organic matter should be added to the ground each fall to serve as a buffer against soil disease.

Never work among plants when the foliage is wet, either from rain or from watering; this can spread disease from leaf to leaf. Don't walk on the ground itself when it's soaking wet, for this compacts the soil and injures roots that are close to the surface. Try also to **diversify the plantings,** even within the rows themselves. No matter how much you enjoy any particular vegetable, don't plant several rows of it close together, corn being the one obvious exception. Certain bugs prefer certain plants, and if there's a large quantity of these susceptible plants close to each other the pest may proliferate much faster than it would if half or even two-thirds of the row were planted with something else.

There is evidence that a virus disease that attacks tomatoes is brought in through the handling of tobacco. If you are a pipe smoker, in spite of all those delightful pictures of elderly gardeners puffing away on their pipes as they bend among their vegetable plants, put the pipe aside and wash your hands before you tie up the tomatoes. Be very careful where you put your feet when working near vining plants that are allowed to run along the ground. Treading on the growing tips of squash or cucumbers or melons not only does serious physical damage but also opens a wound through which disease can enter.

If you are training climbing plants against any kind of solid fence or wall, fasten the wire or netting onto supports that stand at least 12 inches away from the solid surface. I use long shelf brackets on wooden house walls and fences, and string the appropriate cross wires from them. Training the plants away from the wall allows air to circulate behind the vines, which reduces their susceptibility to mildew and their attractiveness to various insect pests.

If you spot **what seems to be a very sick plant, it is wise to pull it out.** A plant that is wilting in early morning might be a case in point. Put it into a plastic bag and send it out with

the trash. I do not put diseased plants in my compost pile, even though I know the internal heat of the compost will eventually destroy the disease spores; since this takes time I prefer to get a plant that is full of mildew or some other disease immediately out of my yard. After handling a diseased plant, always wash your hands before you touch any other plants, and if you dig up a diseased plant, sterilize the tool afterward in a strong mixture of bleach and water.

A large bird population is a great insurance against many plant pests. **Birds** can be attracted and kept around by planting shrubs that provide thick shelter or carry the berries they enjoy. To lure birds more quickly into a new yard, set out feeders and fresh water, winter and summer alike. Water is just as important as food to birds all year long. There are various electrical devices available from seed catalogs to keep ice from forming. If, like me, you don't want to bother with this, add fresh water on top of any ice that forms and on a mild day empty everything out and start afresh. Though birds enjoy the handouts at feeders (and sometimes, considering the cost of bird food, I think they enjoy it too much), they do not give up their natural and endless search for insects. Even when they're free-loading from your plant stand, winter and summer alike, birds consume tens of thousands of insect pests at an incredible rate.

I have not gone into the business of releasing lady bugs, praying mantis, and Trichogramma wasps in my yard, mainly because I have a neighbor who does this all the time, so our place gets the overflow of those **predatory insects** that cannot stake out territory for themselves where they're first released. For those without my good fortune, these insects are beneficial in a yard, as long as they stay around, which is something that no one can control, and with the praying mantis it is well to remember that this is not a discriminatory insect; it will be just as happy eating a bee as it will a cabbage butterfly! Yet these are simple, preventative measures that every vegetable gardener should think about taking. They won't eliminate all the problems, but they will reduce the likelihood of devastating attacks.

Natural Pest-Control Sources

Bio-Control Co., Route 2, Box 2397, Auburn, Calif. 95603
(Lady Bugs and Praying Mantises)

Eastern Bio-Control Co., Route 5, Box 379, Jackson, N.J. 08527
(Praying Mantises)

Fairfax Biological Control Laboratory, Clinton Corners, N.Y.
12514 (Milky Spore Disease, Trade name: Doom)

Ferndale Gardens, 332 Nursery Lane, Faribault, Minn. 55201
(Praying Mantises)

Gothard Inc., Box 370, Cantutillo, Texas 79835 (Trichogramma
wasps and Praying Mantises)

International Minerals & Chemical Corp., Box 192, Libertyville,
Ill. 60048 (Thuricide and Dipel)

Mincemoyer Nursery, County Line Road, Jackson, N.J. 08527
(Praying Mantises)

B. G. Pratt Co., 230 21st Ave., Paterson, N.J. 07509 (Pyrethrum
substitute White Fly spray)

Schnoor's Sierra Bug Co., Box 114, Rough & Ready, Calif. 95975
(Lady Bugs)

Thompson-Hayward Chemical Co., Box 2383, Kansas City,
Kan. 66110 (Biotrol)

Vitova Insectary, Box 475, Rialto, Calif. 92376 (Trichogramma
wasps)

Also check seed company catalogs (see pages 72–73) and the
Montgomery Ward Farm catalog.

There are some specific pests worth advance planning to destroy. The first and worst of these, for northeastern gardeners, is the **Japanese beetle,** which has again become an intolerable nuisance in many gardening areas. There is some slight evidence that the present horrible resurgence of this pest has resulted because its grubs (which winter over in the soil) have become able to tolerate chlordane, which may have been overused in efforts to control the beetles. I have never used

chlordane, but I did use Doom successfully when it first came on the market. Doom is a biological control, known as milky spore disease, that infects the grubs. Milky spore disease not only kills the grubs but leaves a residual effect in the soil, which infects later generations of grubs, and it worked very well for me. It does, however, take time to have a marked effect on the Japanese beetles themselves, and it is the most successful in areas where there is warm soil late into the fall. Doom is sold locally at a great many garden centers. If you cannot get it there, it is worth writing to the Fairfax Biological Control Laboratory (p. 153) for the name of your local distributor. This control is best applied very early in the spring, exactly according to the directions; one application put down very thoroughly around your yard will last for many years.

Snails and slugs are in every garden. If they seem to be experiencing a population explosion, I use poison bait, now that I'm past the stage of having vulnerable grandchildren who put their fingers in their mouths. I lay it down with gloved hands in a cordon sanitaire around the perimeter of the vegetable plot, and I always cover it with small-meshed wire as a safeguard for dogs. The slugs that are already inside the plot before I lay down the bait I hold at bay with sunken saucers of stale beer in which they enthusiastically drown themselves in drunken splendor. An excellent way to pick off the slugs that are devastating your lettuce or your peas is to walk down the row of plants, which you know are being attacked by the slime the slugs leave, at night with a torch and deal with the marauders in a hand-to-hand encounter. If you rise with the birds you can also do it in the morning. There are highly potent slug killers on the market, but they are for use among ornamental plants and come with warnings against using them in the vegetable garden. Be sure to read labels carefully. Some gardeners will not mulch, since they maintain the slugs like to shelter under the mulch by day. This has not been my experience, and in any case the usefulness of mulch far outweighs this possible disadvantage.

Earwigs, which are a great pest in some gardens, have never really troubled us. We have some, and these I trap by

suspending flower pots on stakes upside down in the vegetable garden. The earwigs congregate in them by day and can be shaken off into a bucket of water. There are chemical compounds that will kill earwigs, if they really reach the pest stage, but these I have had no occasion to use.

Ants in a yard are not a problem in themselves, but the aphids they bring as milch cows to plants and plant roots can do great damage. If ants are a nuisance, try to find the ant hills, dig these up, and pour boiling water in them. I watch out for aphids, and if I see them beginning to collect on the tip ends of plants, I try hosing the colonies off with a blast of cold water at high pressure from the hose. This same treatment used on the undersides of the leaves of infested plants works well for **mite** and **red spider,** whose ravages are apparent in the sickly-looking condition of the leaf itself and also in small webs that they leave on the leaves they have attacked. Any hosing that I do always takes place in the morning of a hot day, so the plant foliage can dry off before night. This is particularly important in hot, humid weather, when foliage going wet into the night is often an open road to an attack of mildew. If hosing doesn't work, I dust the plant with either rotenone or pyrethrum dusts which are available everywhere. Sometimes I use an all-purpose spray, also made of these organic compounds. As a result of the questions which have been raised about the effect of freon, the propellant in all aerosol sprays, upon the atmosphere, I am inclined to think I shall give up sprays that have aerosol propellants and concentrate on dusting instead.

I don't have any professional dusting equipment; instead I put some rotenone or pyrethrum dust into the center of a square of cheesecloth, draw up the cheesecloth by the four corners, and then shake the dust out among the foliage of the affected plants, making sure that it gets on the undersides of the leaves as well as on the surface. This treatment will kill aphids, white fly, bean beetles, flea beetles, and most caterpillars. Dusting is, of course, no good if rain immediately follows the treatment; then you will have to dust again. When dusting be sure to tie a scarf over your nose and mouth. If all these efforts fail, very occasionally I will use an oil spray that can be

mixed with water in a glass sprayer that goes on the end of a garden hose. Volck, a miscible oil spray put out by the Ortho Company, works well, but do follow the directions exactly. I resort to this only if the infestations are intolerable, which has happened to me only a couple of times. For minute infestations of aphids an effective home spray can be made by blending fresh hot peppers and commercial red pepper together with two cloves of garlic in a blender with a cup of water. Strain off the liquid, and dilute 50:50 with plain water.

Earlier I mentioned the care that must be taken not to introduce infected plants into a yard from outside; the same thing applies equally forcefully to your own house plants. Do not set out any house plants that are infested with **white fly** (which, unfortunately, most of us recognize only at an advanced stage when clouds of tiny white specks fly up when the plant is touched) anywhere near the vegetable plot, nor hang susceptible plants (like fuchsias, which are appallingly attractive to white flies) near the tomato trellis. Any such action gives this pest a tremendous head start toward becoming almost an intolerable nuisance in the vegetable garden. Plants that are worst infected with white fly are all the cucurbits— that is, squash, zucchini, cucumber, and melon—as well as tomatoes, eggplants, and peppers. Worse still, if a terrible infection of white fly hits your vegetables, their egg masses will winter over happily, even through the coldest weather. White fly that reaches pest proportions in a garden should be handled at the time with summer oil spray, and a dormant oil spray such as Scalecide should be sprayed all over the lot in very early spring in order to destroy the egg masses that may have been left by the past summer outbreak.

Clearance has just been given by the Environmental Protection Agency to new synthetic substitutes for the natural insecticide pyrethrum. These synthetics are more effective against a wide range of insects than the natural substance and will control aphids, Japanese beetles, and Colorado potato beetles, among other insects. One of these synthetics is now available in aerosol form as a white-fly spray but it has not yet been cleared for use on vegetables.

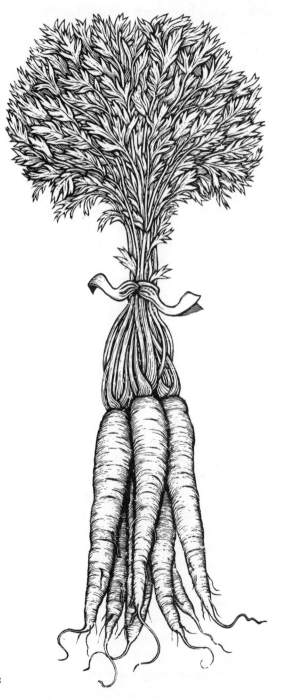

Carrots

In recent years I have been greatly bothered by **cabbage worms,** which attack all my brassica plants and burrow in so deeply that the dustings of rotenone or pyrethrum do not seem to reach them. These I now control with *Bacillus thüringiensis,* a bacterial disease that attacks specific caterpillars, including, very fortunately, the imported cabbage caterpillar. (It is marketed as Thuricide, Biotrol, and Dipel and is available through most garden centers, from seed catalogs, or from manufacturers. See list on p. 153.)

If **caterpillars** are only a slight and occasional nuisance, it is worth trying Ruth Stout's method of shaking a little salt over the infested plants and repeating this after every rainfall. It will work well, just so long as you use a very light dose; too much salt will damage the foliage irreparably. The Trichogramma wasp, which my neighbors release, is supposed to control caterpillars, but I have seen no evidence that they pay the least attention to this pest. If you find a horned tomato worm on your tomatoes covered with white encrustations, take it away from the tomatoes, but don't kill it. The wretched creature is doomed already by the parasites that are feeding on its flesh, and you need these to hatch to serve your garden as protectors in their turn.

A great deal is written these days about pest control through **companion planting,** which can be either setting out a plant that is more attractive to the pests that usually get on the vegetable crops, so they crowd onto the companion plant instead, or else setting out a plant that scares the pests with its smell. Nasturtiums, for example, are enormously attractive to every kind of aphid. If you plant them in sufficient quantities near vegetables that otherwise attract aphids, the aphids will concentrate far more heavily upon the nasturtiums than they will upon vegetable plants. I use climbing or vining nasturtiums among the cucumbers; they happily scramble up the trellis and are instantly overwhelmed with aphids. I read that nasturtiums among cucumbers also repel the cucumber beetle, and it is a fact that my plantings of cucumbers have, to date, not been troubled by beetles. It is also said that dill planted near tomatoes appears to keep away the tomato worm. I have

a great deal of trouble with tomato worms, so perhaps I do not grow enough dill. I have observed that when the sweet-smelling nicotiana, or tobacco plant, which self-seeds like a weed in our yard, appears anywhere near the tomatoes, then the attacks of the tomato worm become even more serious, which might count as companion planting in reverse! So keep nicotiana as far away as possible from your tomatoes.

Plenty of garlic planted around the plot, and, if possible, left in over the winter to turn into really large bulbs, seems to serve as a general pest repellent. There is always much less problem in any section of the yard where garlic is thriving particularly well. Mint and ants don't mix; there is no point in searching for the ant's nest in the mint patch, because it simply won't be there. Unfortunately mint is such a rampant spreader that it cannot be planted at random in a vegetable plot for control of the ants, or it will take over the plot in its own right. Geraniums, particularly white geraniums, which are quite the most difficult to flower well, do attract Japanese beetles, which they seem to stun but not to kill. If you use geraniums as a beetle lure, you must sweep up all the moribund beetles that will be lying on the ground around the plant, before they revive, and dispose of them in some other way. Marigolds are excellent for controlling **root nematodes,** which are microscopically tiny eellike worms that can ruin the roots of crops. I plant the low-growing French variety of marigold at random throughout the vegetable area every summer, and so far I've had no nematode problem at all. A friend of mine also reports that a row of radish seeds sown among cucumbers, squash, and melons will eliminate most of their pests. Of this I to date have no firsthand evidence, but my friend is an excellent horticulturist, so I most certainly mean to try it myself.

As precaution against plant diseases I do nothing except buy protected seeds and protected plants if I am going to set out preraised plants. In thirty years of vegetable gardening I have never had all my crops devastated by any one disease during a single season. Organic gardeners who do wish to spray against the various wilt or fungus diseases can use the old-fashioned Bordeaux mixture of wettable sulfur, which

should, incidentally, never be used anytime when the temperature is above 80 degrees.

Since I do not use the new chemical pest control sprays or dusts, I am not able to give a firsthand account of their efficiency. Talking to my friends who do spray, I have learned that Zineb is an excellent, all-purpose preventative spray for tomatoes, while Methoxychlor is now considered safe and usable for all forms of beetles, cutworms, caterpillars, white fly, and aphids. Malathion, according to the label, can also be used for these same pests.

For **fungicidal disease,** Benlate, which is a form of Benomyl, which is in turn a mildly systemic poisoning, is recommended by one of my vegetable gardening friends. But in view of the recommendations of E.P.A. I personally would prefer not to use this anywhere in my yard. Sevin, which is also on sale in every form in garden centers and through seed catalogs, is an effective pesticide, but it is lethal to bees, and though this fact is made clear on the containers, I am not sure those who use it so freely are always quite aware of what they're doing. It is extremely hard to use Sevin in a vegetable plot without something being in bloom and when there are no bees around. Since the produce that comes to us from our vegetable plot is largely courtesy of the pollination work of bees, the use of Sevin may eliminate a basic link in producing the harvest we hope to gather.

Those who use chemical sprays must read the labels very carefully. Manufacturers are required to list the areas where it is *safe* to use the spray, dust, or concentrate in any form, but they are not required to say where it is unsafe.

> **If there is no specific mention that a particular spray or dust can be used among vegetables, then it is probably unwise to use it there.**

Most manufacturers are extremely careful to make clear when certain sprays are unsafe for use among edible foodstuffs; in some cases they list specific crops on which certain insecticides should not be used. But not everyone is so conscientious, and if there is no mention of the suitability of a certain product in

the vegetable plot, then the gardener should assume it to be unsuitable even if it is listed as controlling an insect pest that is plaguing your vegetables. If you have any doubts about a certain product write to the Environmental Protection Agency, Federal Registration Division, Washington, D.C. 20460.

It is also vital to understand that the drift from any spray that can be used on ornamental plants but is not considered suitable in vegetable plots can be easily carried by the wind onto edible food plants. This is true also of the herbicides used to control weeds. Any that contain 2.4.D. or 2.4.5.7.T. will kill many vegetables and also seriously contaminate the land on which the mist settles. Such spraying should, therefore, be carried out only on a day that is completely windless, something that is amazingly hard to come by. In my opinion it should never be carried out close to a vegetable plot, no matter how calm the day.

With every chemical spray or dust, therefore, it is necessary to read the directions extremely carefully, particularly in relation to the date on which spraying must stop before the crops are harvested. And with any produce that has been sprayed with chemicals, it is absolutely essential that the washing be very thorough.

In general, the novice gardener should not expect to be able to run a vegetable plot without any pest or disease problems, for every year something will happen to some plant. The answer is not the elimination of pests, for this is really impossible without measures that are too strong for the ordinary household possibly to attempt. The trick is to try to live with the pests and minimize them as far as possible by rather simple methods or by very judicious uses of sprays or dusts, and also by eliminating infected plants before they spread their problem elsewhere. To my mind this is still the best way to tackle plant pests and diseases in the home plot, particularly if you are new to the game and are not really quite sure what you are doing. If we think of plant pests and diseases in terms of remaining in control of the situation, rather than eradicating every possible disability, then we will be taking the balanced view that leads to good gardening.

How to Grow Specific Vegetables

In this list it is assumed *either* that the land was fall-prepared in the manner discussed on pages 39, 41–43 and needs no extra spring fertilizer unless specifically mentioned *or* that if the grounds are being got ready for the first time in the spring, or if the vegetables are not to be grown under perpetual mulch, at least two inches of organic matter and five pounds of 5-10-5 or 5-10-10 fertilizer will be incorporated into every 100 square feet of land in very early spring just as soon as the ground is workable.

The varieties mentioned are the ones that I use and the ones used by gardening friends.

ASPARAGUS

A perennial plant that, properly set out and cared for, will produce for ten to twenty years. Two trenches containing 25 plants each will produce a reasonable crop for small plots.

Culture

The trenches should be in a well-drained sunny position, and there should be as much wind protection as possible. The site should be as far as possible from trees, for, otherwise, the roots will work their way into the bed. Each side of, but totally separate from, the vegetable plot is an excellent place. As-

paragus will thrive only where there is sufficient winter cold or long dry period to kill the top growth and ensure complete dormancy for the roots.

1st year

Fall: Dig or rototill trenches 2 feet wide and 12 inches deep. If they are to be side by side, leave 3 feet between the beds. Remove the loosened soil and pile it alongside the entire length of the trenches. Spread a 6-inch layer of half-decomposed compost or well-rotted manure, if this is available, or any other form of organic matter along the bottom of the trench and dig this in. Leave the trenches open all winter.

1st year

Very early spring: Order asparagus plants through seed catalogs or garden centers. Before these arrive, spread 3 pounds of 5-10-5 fertilizer for every 25 feet of row along the bottom of the trench and work this in with a spade. Pull an inch of unfertilized soil over the fertilized soil from the mound beside the trench and trample this down so that the bottom of the trench is firm and flat, but not pounded down into a cementlike surface! Unpack the plants carefully, being very careful of the brittle roots. Keep them covered with a piece of damp sacking once they are taken outside. Set the plants 18 inches apart in the center of the bottom of the trench. The plants should be set out with the crown or bud upward, and the roots carefully spread out in every direction. Cover each plant immediately with 2 inches of soil from the mound. Do not wait to cover the plants until the whole row is laid out; this wait can lead to fatal root drying out. When all the plants are covered, firm the soil around them lightly with your hands. Do not use the back of the hoe or your feet; the roots are too brittle.

1st year

Spring: As the plant shoots develop, slowly fill in the trench until all the mounded-up soil is used and the fill is level with surrounding ground. If the trench is lower than the surrounding area after all the stored soil is in, add more earth to top it up. Once the trench is filled, mulch heavily around the plants to smother weeds.

1st year

Summer: Little or no harvesting should be done the first

year, and great care should be taken to preserve all the foliage. Staking with thin bamboo canes is advisable in very windy locations. For a good crop the subsequent spring, asparagus roots always need plenty of healthy foliage for the entire growing season. If the soil feels dry under the mulch, water the beds thoroughly. As the summer mulch shrinks it should be regularly renewed.

1st year

Midsummer: Scatter a band of 5-10-10 fertilizer on each side of the trench in a band 8 inches wide at the rate of 1 pound per 25 feet of row. Keep this fertilizer 6 inches away from the edge of the trench. Cultivate it in and water thoroughly. Then cover this area with a thick mulch.

1st year

Fall: When frost kills the top growth, cut it off at the ground level and add it to the compost pile, and pull out any weeds that may have grown into the mulch. Spread 2 inches of half-decayed compost over the summer mulch, and cover this with leaves held down by chicken wire.

2nd and subsequent years

Every year the asparagus beds will need two feedings. The first should take place in very early spring, when the mulch should be pulled back to warm up the soil, and 5 pounds of 5-10-10 fertilizer should be mixed into the topsoil of every 25 feet of trench. The second application should follow the method outlined above and should be done as soon as the cutting season is ended.

Harvesting

2nd year

In the second season, harvest shoots 7 inches tall for a month, and then stop cutting.

Subsequent years

Harvest all shoots from now on except those that are very thin. Do not cut the stalks with a knife under the soil surface; this can damage unseen shoots. Harvest by bending the stalks so that they snap. This method produces fully edible stalks. (The tough, white uneatable portions of stalks on commercially grown asparagus have been severed well below soil surface level.) Stop harvesting when all the stalks diminish in size,

and allow these to turn into the fernlike foliage. In well-planted, well-fertilized beds it may be necessary to harvest daily when the stalks are appearing in quantity to keep the bed in strong production.

Ailments

Very little troubles asparagus, but watch out for slugs which love it. Rust can be eliminated by purchasing rust-resistant varieties. If the asparagus beetle appears it can be controlled with rotenone. For consistent lavish production, asparagus beds must be kept weed-free. If mulch is not used, the beds must be hand-weeded all summer. Weed growth is likely to be very heavy, owing to the regular use of fertilizer, but cultivating with a hoe is difficult without injuring the essential foliage.

Varieties

Martha Washington, Waltham Washington.

BASIL

This is an easily grown annual herb that has many culinary uses, particularly, of course, with tomatoes. Both leaves and flowers can be used, but it's more usual to pinch out the flowers and to pick only the leaves.

Culture

Basil is easily grown from seed indoors and then transplanted, or outdoors planted half an inch deep as soon as the soil warms up. It needs full sun, but it will tolerate a slightly shady position. The soil should not be fertilized, as basil will be less aromatic if grown in rich soil. When the soil is extremely rich, basil will readily grow 2 feet in height, but for most plots a smaller, more compact plant is more useful. Plants should be set 12 inches apart if the soil is very good. Sow seeds in pots in late summer; outdoor plants seldom take kindly to being potted and brought indoors.

Ailments

Aphids occasionally attack basil but are easily hosed off, and white fly can be a nuisance.

Varieties

Sweet basil and a bush basil that has a more compact form

and is slightly more aromatic. *Dark Opal* is less tasty but more decorative and can be used in flower gardens.

BEANS

Beans are vegetables that with few exceptions, purple bush beans and broad or fava beans, need warm soil to germinate. They are also extremely susceptible to the least touch of air frost. Very early young shoots should be protected if there is the least likelihood of frost, and late-season shell beans that are ripening on the vines or bushes must also be protected from an early frost. Beans cannot be transplanted, except if grown in well-moistened peat pots, and should be sown where they are to grow. All beans add nitrogen to the soil, so fertilizers with a high nitrogen count should not be used with beans, or there will be an overabundance of foliage at the expense of the crop.

Bush Beans, Green and Wax (yellow)
Culture

Early spring: With the exception of purple-pod bush beans, which can be planted two weeks earlier, bush beans are best sown in ground that has warmed up about a week before the average date of the last spring frost. For those who garden under mulch, the mulch should be drawn back to expose the soil to the sun's warmth for two weeks before the seed is sown. Bush beans should be sown in short rows with 2 feet between the rows. Bean seed should go in a furrow 1 inch deep, 2 to 3 inches apart, and be thinned to stand 4 inches apart. Midsummer and late sowings should go into furrows 2 inches deep. Not more than an inch of soil should cover the seed in either case. If the soil is clay and tends to crust, the seed should be covered with vermiculite. Bean furrows should be kept well watered until the seed has broken through the ground. As the sprouts straighten up and unfurl their true leaves the mulch should be drawn up closely to them. Successive plantings can be made every two weeks up to six weeks before the average date of the first fall frost. The time between plantings should decrease from 2 weeks to 11 days as the season progresses.

Succession crops

Where beans are grown as a succession crop in well-prepared land there is usually no need of extra fertilizer, for their needs are different from the crop they follow. If the shoots remain pale and stunted, the mulch should be removed and a 6-inch band of 5-10-5 or 5-10-10 fertilizer should be spread like a dusting of heavy snow on each side of the row, but 6 inches away from the plants—do not allow it to touch the stems or leaves of the beans. Rake fertilizer in and water carefully but thoroughly, then put back the mulch. A safer but more costly method is to mix ½ cup of slow-release timed fertilizer into the soil where the bean seed is to go. But this will be needed only in poor soil.

Harvesting

Bush and wax beans should be harvested while they are still young and will snap when bent. Unless the pods are harvested when they are ready the plant will stop bearing. Well-grown bush or wax beans in soil which has been kept properly moist should produce for at least two weeks as long as all large tough pods are regularly removed.

Ailments

These are the same for all types of beans. Do not work among beans or even pick them when the foliage is wet; this spreads disease. For spotted Mexican bean beetles rotenone or pyrethrum is a safe insecticide; but make sure it reaches the underside of the leaves where the egg masses are clustered. Beans grown in well-prepared soil that receive plenty of moisture are rarely attacked by this nuisance. If malathion is used, wait two weeks before harvesting.

Varieties

Very early: *Royalty Purple Pod.* Normal planting time: **Green**— *Tenderette, Tendercrop, Top Crop, Bush Romano.* For gardens with a short growing season: *Contender, Black Valentine.* **Wax**— *Brittle Wax, Pencil Pod, Kinghorn.* Short season: *Eastern Butterwax.*

Pole Beans

These are the climbing varieties of bush beans. Well-grown, the vines will reach 6 feet in height, except Romano, which will stay around 4 to 5 feet.

Culture

Pole beans can be sown only once in a season, and they should not go into the ground until two weeks after the bush beans. Grown on a trellis (pages 64–65), they should be sown 1 inch deep and 2 inches apart and subsequently thinned to stand 4 inches apart. Pole beans can also be grown up rough poles with the bark still on them, sunk deeply into the ground, or up tepees made by setting three poles into the ground in a triangle and tying them together at the top. Six seeds should be planted around each pole and thinned to the three strongest. Climbing beans often need help to get started upward; the elongating stem should be wound very carefully with a couple of twists *clockwise* around the support.

Very early spring: To bear continuously over the growing season, pole beans need a heavy supply of nutrients. To get the ground ready for them, the area where they are to grow should have 5-10-5 or 5-10-10 fertilizer incorporated into it at the rate of 1 pound for every 25 feet of row. Pole beans will crop heavily about two and a half months after they were sown, if the weather has been warm and they have received plenty of moisture. To make sure of continuous production all the pods must be harvested as they reach an edible size. If the supply seems to be diminishing, extra fertilizer in the same proportion can be added in a furrow 6 inches from the plants or in a ring around the growing poles and watered in well. Pole beans grow best with a thick water-conserving mulch covering the ground around them.

Varieties

Earliest: *Romano.* Midseason: *Kentucky Wonder, Blue Lake.* For cooler areas: *Scarlet Runner* (see page 92).

Lima Bush Beans

Lima beans are a single-season crop and not suited to short-season gardening. I have grown limas successfully in Zone 5, but only in years when spring has come very early.

Culture

Lima beans should not be planted until the soil is thoroughly warmed up, around the time the tomatoes and cucumbers are set out. They take two and a half months of

warm weather to crop, and if the season is cool or wet the crop will be still further delayed. They also will not crop in areas where the temperatures remain extremely high during the summer growing season. I would not suggest them for the novice grower with a small plot. For those who have the space or the climate to grow them, lima beans do not like overrich soil, so go easy on the fertilizer. They should be planted 1 inch deep and thinned to stand 10 inches apart. The plants need plenty of room to bear well.

Ailments
Should tiny holes begin to appear in the leaves, dust immediately with rotenone.

Varieties
Those most consistently recommended are: *Fordhook 242, Baby Fordhook, Henderson Thaxter.*

Lima Pole Beans
Lima pole beans are a better crop than bush limas for the small home gardener, for they produce more in a smaller space. They are very strong climbers, and the supports have to be very deeply set into the ground. They take very nearly three months in ideal growing conditions to come to harvest.

Variety
King of the Garden.

Fava or Broad Beans
This is a bean a little larger than a lima in size, with a highly distinctive flavor. It also takes nearly three months to crop, but since fava beans demand cool growing conditions and cool soil, they are an excellent bean for short-season areas. Fava beans are considered a particular delicacy by Europeans. The crop will last in cool climates about a month.

Culture
Early spring: Fava beans should be planted as early as the ground can be worked. They need deeper planting than other beans, around 3 inches deep, and about 5 inches apart. They should be thinned to stand 9 inches apart with the rows 2 feet

apart. Like pole beans they need extra fertilizer, in the same proportions. Fava beans grow on a tall single stalk. Some growers pinch out the top when the plants reach a height of 3 feet, so that they will need no staking.

Ailments

Fava or broad beans are very susceptible to black aphids and to black fly. These can be controlled by rotenone or pyrethrum or other sprays.

Varieties

H.S. Long Pod, British *Imperial Green Windsor.* The catalog of the English seedsmen Thompson and Morgan carries a variety of broad or fava beans.

Horticultural or Shell Beans

For the small gardener there is rarely enough room to grow horticultural shell beans as a separate crop. If the family's interest in dried or whole beans is very great, then these can be obtained by allowing bush beans or pole beans to mature and using these. Home-raised beans that are to be stored as dried beans should be shelled and placed on a cookie sheet in a slow oven (130–145 degrees) for one hour to kill any weevils that might have burrowed into them.

BEETS

Beets can be sown as soon as the ground is workable, though in the Northeast it is inadvisable to put them in earlier than April 15. Beets are a bellwether plant in a vegetable garden. If they do well, the chances are excellent that all the other plantings will thrive.

Culture

Beets need well-raked soil that is free of clods and stones to a depth of 8 inches. If the soil has not been tested, and yours is an area where rhododendrons flourish, a scattering of ground limestone like a light dusting of snow, well raked into the soil a week ahead where beets are to be sown, is a wise precaution.

Very early spring: Each seed consists of a cluster of three or four seeds, so the beets will germinate in little clumps. The seed should be sown in furrows ½ inch deep, about 1 inch apart. The rows, which should be short, can be 10 inches apart. Seed should be covered with ½ inch of soil. When the seedlings are 2 inches tall, thin by clipping at soil level to one plant per inch. When they reach 4 inches in height, thin to 4 inches apart. The second thinnings can be transplanted by the mud method (pages 108–9), or you can wait a little longer and use them as beet greens.

All summer: Additional sowings of beets can be made every two weeks up to two months before the average date of the first fall frost; many growers prefer to concentrate on spring and late summer sowings. In very hot weather the seed will not germinate unless it is sown in a furrow 1 inch deep and covered lightly with vermiculite which is kept regularly moistened. For quick, succulent growth, beets, like all vegetables, need a regular supply of moisture around the roots. For that reason, the rows should be thickly mulched after a thorough ground watering.

Harvesting

Beets taste best harvested when the roots have expanded to about 2 inches across. Most beets toughen up during hot weather; one variety, *Long Season,* stays succulent through summer heat.

Ailments

Very little troubles beets if the ground is properly prepared. If the seed was sown very early and the temperature remains below 40 degrees for a couple of weeks after the seed had germinated the plants may bolt—that is, run to seed rather than form an edible root. In that case use the beet greens and resow. If the leaves are stunted and lack green color, there may be a phosphorus deficiency in the soil and a feeding of 5-10-5 fertilizer would be beneficial.

Beet leaves are susceptible to attack from leaf miners and webworm. These can be controlled with pyrethrum.

Varieties

Early Wonder, Detroit Dark Red, Crosby, and *Long Season.*

Beets

BROCCOLI

This plant is a member of the cabbage family (also known as cole or brassica). It is extremely hardy, and young plants properly hardened off (pages 143–45) can be set outdoors while the ground is still cold and there is still danger of air frost. Fall broccoli will continue to produce after the first frosts until the day temperature falls below freezing. This is an excellent plant for the small plot, since it is not a one-time harvest but stays in production in cool weather for well over two months.

Culture

6 weeks before the last spring frost: Sow seed indoors (pages 135 ff.) and grow the seedlings in as cool and bright a place as possible. Two weeks before the plants go out, the ground where they are to be planted should receive additional spring fertilizer, 1 pound of 5-10-10 or ½ cup of a timed-release fertilizer for every 25 feet of row. The fertilizer should be worked well into the topsoil.

If the soil was not fall-tested, and if you live where rhododendrons flourish, rake in a sprinkling of ground horticultural lime like light snow as the gound is being prepared. This will reduce the acidity and make the soil more alkaline and therefore more compatible with plants of the cabbage family.

Spring: The seedlings should be set 2 feet apart and should be immediately protected from cutworms (pages 107–8). The area where they are growing should be thickly mulched. If there is a prolonged period without rain, water the ground slowly and very deeply through the mulch. Buds will start to set about two months after the plants go outdoors.

Midsummer: Either start more broccoli seedlings under fluorescent lights, or in a cold frame, or sow a short row ½ inch deep with the seed covered with vermiculite in the plot. Thin the seedlings to stand 1 inch apart soon after germination and keep well protected against cabbageworm and aphids (see below). Seedlings of the brassica family are not affected by heat at this immature stage and can be safely grown on until they are 5 inches tall or have four to five true leaves, when they should be moved to a position where root crops, such as carrots, have already been harvested. The soil should

be refreshed with 2 inches of organic matter and the proportion of fertilizer mentioned above, dug in before fall broccoli is set out. If the plot is large, the midsummer seeding can be done in the row where the plants are to grow, and the seedlings gradually thinned to stand about 2 feet apart. When the nights start to cool off, the plants will spurt ahead and begin to set heads. These should be harvested in exactly the same way as the spring crop. Edible side shoots will continue to form for many subsequent weeks.

Harvesting

Harvest the main head while the buds are still bright green and tight; extra buds will form as side shoots as long as the weather remains under 70 degrees at night. If the plant ceases producing, it should be pulled out. It will start to throw fresh side shoots in fall weather, but it is not worth allowing it to take up so much space for so long.

Ailments

Brassicas are affected by several soil-borne diseases; for that reason it is extremely important always to change the place where the crop is raised, but above all, always to buffer the soil with plenty of fresh organic matter before setting out new plants. In all my years of vegetable growing, because of this simple precaution I have never suffered from any of the brassica soil problems or even from soil maggots. (See pages 99, 101.) Aphids, and green worms hatched from the eggs of cabbage butterflies, always are a nuisance, especially to young plants. Aphids should be washed off with a hard stream of water from the hose as soon as they are spotted. Worms can be controlled with rotenone or *Bacillus thüringiensis*. Malathion can be safely used on young plants, but if used after the heads have started to form, wait two weeks before harvesting.

Varieties

Early: *Cleopatra, Green Comet.* Fall: *Waltham 2, Calabrese.*

BRUSSELS SPROUTS

This member of the brassica family is best grown only as a fall crop except in cool, short-season areas. It is well worth

the space it takes up even in small plots, since it bears small edible heads for weeks on end, long after frost has finished off other green vegetables. Fresh hárvested sprouts that have had a taste of frost are sweet and tender and worthy of much more appreciation than they receive! Brussels sprouts should not be grown where other members of the brassica or cole family have been planted earlier in the season.

Culture

June: Handle the seed exactly like the midsummer crop of broccoli.

Fall: Brussels sprouts will start to form heads three months after the plants are set out, but only if the night temperature is regularly in the low sixties. Brussels sprouts need moist soil and do better with a mulch. If an early crop is needed, pinch off the growing tip of the plant soon after Labor Day: this will speed up crop production, which will all be ready at approximately the same time, but will diminish the yield tremendously. Left unpinched, Brussels sprouts will start to bear about three weeks later than the pinched plants, but will continue to produce edible heads for a month after the night temperatures fall well below freezing.

I read that if snow is expected, or if both day and night temperatures fall regularly below 20 degrees unexpectedly early in the season, the plants can be lifted with some soil attached and stood upright in a cold garage or cellar and will continue to crop for several weeks. Of this I have no personal experience.

As tiny sprouts start to form along the lower portion of the main stem, pull aside the mulch and scatter a 6-inch band of 5-10-10 like a heavy dusting of snow on both sides of the plant. Do not rake this in, for, like all brassicas, Brussels sprouts are shallow-rooted. Water well, and then re-cover with the mulch.

Harvesting

The heads or sprouts form in the axils of the leaves where they are attached to the main stalk. They are ready to harvest when they are hard and firm. As the first sprouts increase in size, pull off the lower leaves carefully with a downward twist-

ing motion. Often the lower leaves will turn yellow when the sprouts are ready and should be removed anyway, but for bigger sprouts it is wiser to remove the leaves while they are still green to provide more space. But do this only when the sprouts reach 1/2 inch across. Leaves should be slowly stripped off the main stem as the sprouts develop from the bottom upward. The top tuft of leaves should always be left untouched: these leaves are essential for a prolonged harvest.

Ailments

The same as all the brassica family: see "Broccoli."

Varieties

Jade Cross F1, Long Island Improved.

CABBAGE

Cabbage is generally labeled as the most important member of the cole or brassica family, which leads novice gardeners to conclude that it is the perfect crop to grow in a small plot. This has not been my experience. Cabbage is, it is true, a crop that produces over a long period, particularly if early, midseason, and late varieties are grown. But once a cabbage head is cut, that is the end of it unless you are prepared to wait around and see whether the miserable stump will throw up a few small cabbage heads, which does occasionally happen. In terms of productiveness, cabbage rates far behind broccoli or Brussels sprouts for the owners of small plots in relation to the time and space it occupies. I would not advise a novice gardener with limited space to grow more than a single row of fall cabbage.

Culture

Cabbage particularly dislikes acid soil. Unless you are very sure that your soil tests between 6.0 and 7.5 in the pH scale, ground limestone must be worked into the soil where cabbage plants are to be set out. Powdering it on like a heavy dusting of snow and raking it in will do the job. To form good heads, cabbage also requires a great deal of nutrients. Unless you know from soil testing that your plot is extremely rich, the ground where cabbage is to grow should have 3 inches of organic matter as well as 1 pound of 10-10-10 fertilizer

worked into it for every 25 feet of row. Cabbage in poor to average soil also needs a monthly fertilizing program. A 6-inch band of 10-10-10, spread at the rate of 1/2 pound for each 10 feet of row beside each plant and well watered in, will not be too much. Cabbage needs a constant supply of water to develop well, but the root system is very near the soil surface. Soil moisture should, therefore, be retained and weeds kept down with a mulch rather than cultivating with a hoe.

I do not like enormous heads of cabbage: I find they split easily in hot weather, and they are much too big for our small family to use. Since our soil under perpetual mulch is very rich, I give no extra fertilizer after preparing the soil — and I harvest excellent heads!

Very early spring: Six weeks before the ground is workable outdoors, or eight weeks ahead of the average date of the last frost, start seeds indoors (pages 135 ff.) and grow plants slowly in as cool a place as possible. Cabbage seedlings should have a short thick main stem before they go outdoors. Plants with very skinny stems sometimes run to flower rather than form heads. For spring growing choose early varieties. As soon as the ground is workable, set the home-grown or prestarted plants outside and protect from cutworms (see pages 107–8).

May–June: Sow seed of late cabbage (see "Broccoli" for details). If more heads appear ready to come to harvest than the family can absorb at once, give the main stalks of some of the plants a half twist. This will break some roots and slow down development. Early cabbage is prone to split in summer heat. Checking the growth in this manner sometimes averts splitting.

Ailments
The same as all the other members of the brassica family (see "Broccoli"), but since cabbageworms once deeply entrenched in the cabbage head are hard to reach, early dusting with *Bacillus thüringiensis* or rotenone, repeated after every rain, is extremely important.

Varieties
Early: *Jersey, Wakefield, Stonehead.* Red cabbage: *Ruby Ball.* Late: *Autumn Marvel, Penn, Savoy King.* In short-season areas only early varieties of cabbage should be grown even for fall crops.

CARROTS

Carrots need a well-worked soil that has been raked clear of stones and clods of earth to a depth of at least 8 inches.

Culture

Early spring: Sow the seed 1/4 inch deep in short furrows about 6 feet long and 15 inches apart. Try to space the seeds about five to an inch. When the seed is in the ground and before the earth is drawn back over it, pour boiling water straight from the kettle on it. Cover with 1/2 inch of soil and firm down. Sow new rows every three weeks until two months before the first fall frost. Carrots in the ground will not be harmed by frost; in fact, their taste will be sweetened and improved. But as the ground chills off they will cease to grow, though they can be safely left in this natural storage.

Midsummer: From midsummer on, carrot seeds should be sown 1/2 inch deep and always be covered with a thin layer of vermiculite. As seedlings develop, thin to 1 inch apart. Then when the tops of the carrot roots touch, thin again to 5 inches apart. Carrots need to be kept weed free and well mulched. To harvest, press down before you pull up.

Ailments

Misshapen roots come from ill-prepared ground and from overcrowding. Green shoulders result from not covering the carrots with soil or mulch. Very few pests bother carrots.

Varieties

Long: *Nantes.* Standard: *Chantenay.* Short: *Short 'n Sweet.*

CAULIFLOWER

This is the hardest of the cole/brassica family for the novice gardener to bring to a successful harvest. The plants take up a lot of room for a long period and do not necessarily repay the amount of trouble that has to be taken with them. I would suggest not trying them the first year of vegetable growing and growing them only as a fall crop when the first attempt is made. If you try any, try the Purple Head variety.

Culture

The soil, fertilizer, and water needs of cauliflower are exactly the same as those needed for cabbages. Cauliflower is

nowhere as hardy as cabbage, and if it is to be grown as a spring crop, home-started seedlings or prestarted plants should not be set out until around the date of the late spring frost.

June: For a fall crop, follow the cultural directions for broccoli, but remember that cauliflower needs the extra fertilizer required by cabbages in average or poor soil. The plants should be in their final growing place by mid-July. Cauliflower will not start to head up in hot weather. The plants will also receive a serious, possibly fatal check where heading is concerned if the roots run short of water. A heavy mulch is a necessity with cauliflower even if the rest of the plot is not mulched.

Harvesting

When the flower bud or curd shows as a small white button, the outer leaves of the plant should be gathered together and tied loosely over the curd to keep out the light. Cauliflower should be harvested before the curd begins to separate into individual flowerets. The purple cauliflower which turns green with cooking has a more delicate taste rather like broccoli. This variety is easier to handle than the white, for it needs no tying up. It does, however, take longer to mature than some of the early white varieties.

Ailments

The same as all the other brassicas (see "Broccoli").

Varieties

Snowball, Purple Head.

CELERIAC

This turnip-rooted celery is grown in exactly the same manner as celery proper (following). Dig it when the root ball is about 4 inches across. Like carrots and beets it can be stored in damp sand.

Varieties

Marble Ball, Alabaster, Large Smooth Prague.

CELERY

This is not an easy plant for home gardeners. I have not grown it, though I watched it grow for many years in my

family's garden. Celery in the wild grows in marshy spots, an indication that the cultivated plants need far more moisture than most vegetables. It is also a crop that takes up garden space from early June until frost.

Culture

Fall or early spring: In order to provide celery with the moisture and rich soil it needs, a trench should be made, in exactly the same way as is described under "Asparagus." Celery can stand very cold weather if it is banked—that is to say, soil is drawn up against it as it grows during the summer and hay piled over it once the cold weather sets in. Thus, the work involved in digging such a trench is worth the long-term results it gives the celery. The growing area within the trench should be rich in organic matter and also contain 5-10-10 fertilizer at the rate of 2 1/2 pounds for every 25 feet of row. The organic matter and the fertilizer should be thoroughly incorporated and mixed very well into the topsoil thrown into the bottom of the trench in order to avoid burning if chemical fertilizer is used. Celery is another case in which an organic fertilizer is probably the better choice, even though 5 pounds of this will be needed for every 25 feet of row. If chemical fertilizers are decided upon, the trench must be prepared two weeks before the plants are to be set out and must be thoroughly watered three or four times.

Three months before last spring frost: Sow the seed indoors and use the boiling water treatment on them (page 97). Celery is a relation of parsley and can stand the same handling. Celery will take from ten to twelve weeks growing indoors before it will reach the size of about 3 inches, when it is possible to transplant it into the garden after properly hardening it off.

Late spring: Novice gardeners who want to grow celery would be wise to buy prestarted plants at a garden center and set these out 6 inches apart in the center of a trench, water them thoroughly, and never allow them to wilt. Nor should the celery beds be allowed to lack for water when well established. Celery, therefore, will do best under a heavy mulch.

Harvesting

Dig or pull out the plants and cut roots off just below the

base. You can also harvest single stalks from the outside of the head.

Varieties

Burpee Fordhook, Giant Pascal. Both are unblanched or green celery but can be blanched. Blanching is a complicated process, hardly worthwhile with the tender new green varieties available.

CHARD, SWISS

This is a particularly simple, very productive vegetable for the novice gardener or the owner of a small plot. A close relative of the beet, chard is grown only for the edible leaves and leaf stalks. The plants grow larger and taller than beets. Chard need be sown only once in the plot, for a single row will produce all season; even during the hottest weather it will not bolt to a flower stalk in its first year. In mild climates chard that has wintered over will, however, try to flower the second year; to keep it forming productive leaves, cut off the flower head. It is, in fact, better to sow chard seed fresh each year. Chard is very hardy and untroubled by the first fall frosts. If it is lightly mulched with hay it can often be harvested up to Christmas even in cold climates.

Culture

Seed, which is multiple like beet seed, should be sown around the date of the last spring frost 1 inch deep and 3 inches apart with an inch of soil on top, but it is worth taking a chance and sowing chard as soon as the ground is workable. As the clusters of seedlings appear, thin to stand 6 inches apart, leaving the strongest plants. When the plants touch, pull every other one out. The pulled plants will be edible.

Harvesting

Chard leaves are delicious at a very early, tender stage, and they should always be cut, not pulled. The crop can be harvested in two ways: either by cutting off the outer leaves while allowing new leaves to develop in the center of the plant or by cutting the whole plant an inch above soil level. Treated in the latter fashion, new leaves will eventually reappear, but much

more slowly, and the remaining roots should be immediately watered very thoroughly with a light dose of water-soluble fertilizer. Chard grows best surrounded by a thick mulch. If you have to go away for over a week, it is as well to make a point of removing all big, outside leaves of the chard, leaving nothing but the tiny central leaves; unless this is done the plant will cease to produce. If the plant becomes unproductive, or if the leaves are neither succulent nor very large, nitrogen fertilizer should be spread alongside the row and thoroughly raked in. Nitrogen fertilizers in the form of cottonseed meal or dried blood sprinkled like a dusting of light snow are always an excellent pickup for all leafy crops. The rhubarb chard not only tastes excellent, but the leaf is very handsome in the growing plot and is greatly beloved by flower arrangers.

Ailments

Chard has very few ailments that trouble it. If leaf miners that tunnel through the leaves attack the plants pick those particular leaves off and burn them, or send them out with the rubbish in a plastic bag.

Varieties

Fordhook Giant, Rhubarb Chard, Lucullus.

CHINESE CABBAGE

Chinese cabbage needs a little understanding, for this cool-weather crop with rather specific soil needs is not as well known as it should be to vegetable growers. Because it is not easy to grow in the spring and get a harvest before the summer heat causes it to bolt into seed, novice gardeners would do better to grow it as a fall crop. The outer leaves are usually rather tough and should be discarded at harvest time. The inner leaves of the loose type or the head of the compact variety can be eaten either raw in a salad or cooked, and make a pleasant change from the usual run of fall greens.

Culture

Midsummer: The ground needs excellent preparation. If the soil is poor, or if a previous crop has been harvested where the Chinese cabbage is to grow, 2 inches of fresh compost and

2 pounds of 5-10-10 should be deeply dug in for every 25 feet of row. Seed should be sown from midsummer on in the place where the plants are to mature. Loose-leaved varieties can be used before they are fully ready. Either type takes around two and one-half months to reach full size. Sow the seeds 1/2 inch deep and about 1 inch apart; cover with vermiculite. When the seedlings are 2 inches tall, thin them to stand 6 inches apart. When the leaves touch again, thin them to stand 18 inches apart. If the seed is sown under lights, use individual peat pots for each seedling, sow three to a pot, and then thin by clipping down to the strongest specimen. Set them out in their final growing position within four weeks; any crowding under lights will gear the plants toward forming flower stalks rather than vegetative growth.

Ailments

The same as for all the brassica-cole family (see "Broccoli"), but flea beetles are also likely to attack Chinese cabbage. Regular dusting with rotenone will eliminate these nuisances. If malathion is used, wait fourteen days before harvesting.

Varieties

Loose leaf: *Pac Choy.* Heading: *Wang Bok, Michihli, Burpee Hybrid, Early Hybrid, Wintertime.*

CHIVES

Chives are a long-lived perennial plant that should be grown along the sunny edge of the vegetable plot where they will not interfere with fall and spring soil preparation. In late spring, plantings of chives will flower, after which the foliage and flower stems should be lightly trimmed back.

Culture

Chives, which are not particular about soil, can be introduced into the plot from small pots sold in food markets in the spring. The foliage should be cut back hard and the roots set into the ground rather more deeply than they grew before. The plants of chives should then be thoroughly watered, and in no time fresh green shoots, which are immediately harvestable, will spring up.

Very early spring: Chives can also be grown from seed planted 1/2 inch deep and lightly covered, but usually do not send up enough growth to be worth clipping the first year. Chives should be divided every third year when they first appear in early spring. The clump can be dug up, cut into two or three pieces with a sharp knife, and immediately replanted. There will be very little setback from this treatment. When clumps of chives are being divided in this way it is also possible to plant one clump in a pot and bury the pot in the soil beside the other clumps. Chives can also be grown in containers or window boxes in sunny positions.

Midsummer: When the supply of new shoots diminishes, cut the chives to the ground and water heavily, then scratch or dig a light sprinkling of 5-10-10 around each plant. This will produce a fresh spurt of growth.

Winter: Clumps of chives can be lifted and potted up for winter use, or the pot that was buried in the summer can be dug up. This should be done as late in the fall as possible, and the plants well watered after the potting up. They should be left in an unheated place until they have been subjected to several weeks of hard frost. After that the pots can be brought to a sunny windowsill indoors where the chives will start at once into fresh growth.

Ailments

None worth worrying about. Onion ailments will also attack chives. Watch out for root maggots in grocery-store pots.

COLLARDS AND KALE

Collards and kale are the greens which anyone of British extraction swears he will never eat again once he leaves his homeland! It's not Brussels sprouts that produce those fearful greens of the winter English culinary scene, but rather the boiled, slimy leaves of collard and kale. But there is no need for this unpleasant taste. Properly handled each has an individual and distinctive taste, and, though for many years I refused to grow either of them, I've now taken to regrowing the useful and very productive collard. Collards and kale are mem-

bers of the brassica-cole family, but neither forms any kind of head. Collards grow upright, not unlike a tall budless broccoli, and in rich soil the plants can reach a height of nearly 3 feet. In average soil a height of 2 feet is more usual. Kale grows about two feet tall.

Culture

The culture and soil requirements of collards and kale are exactly the same as for cabbage. They do their best in soil well buffered with organic matter and extra fertilizer.

Very early spring: Sow seed outdoors an inch in depth and about an inch apart as soon as the soil can be worked. Cover with half an inch of soil. As the seedlings emerge, thin gradually until the plants stand 2 feet apart. Protect against cutworms (pages 107–8). If the growing area is a very windy one, set stakes into the ground early where plants have to be thinned and tie the main stems of the remaining plants to the stakes. The final, large thinnings are edible and delicious. Collards and kale are surface rooters and need plenty of moisture, so they grow best with thick mulch.

June: If the plot is a large one, sow a second crop for a fall harvest. These plants are tastier after being touched by light frost, which will not kill them. Kale is even hardier than collards. For a good second crop it is, therefore, perhaps better to sow kale, which will remain unmoved by the bitterest weather and can be harvested perfectly crisp and juicy even when there is snow on the ground.

Harvesting

Leaves can be eaten raw in salads or cooked like cabbage after two months' growth. Kale usually takes two months to mature and collards two and one-half. Try never to harm the growing tip of collards, for the new leaves appear only as the central stem elongates.

Ailments

Identical with all the cabbage family (see "Broccoli"). The leaves should be kept well dusted with rotenone against the ravages of the cabbageworm.

Varieties

Collards: *Georgia.* Kale: *Vates,* or *Dwarf Blue Curled.*

CORN

Corn can be grown in two ways. Three varieties—early, midseason, and late—can all be sown at the same time to bring a succession of crops, and many excellent gardeners do manage their corn this way. The other method, which worked better for me, was to sow an early variety every three weeks in order to keep the crop coming. Corn will develop only when the night temperature and the soil warms up. It is difficult, therefore, to specify when successive plantings should be made; it might be better to suggest that a second planting go into the ground as soon as the first planting is 3 inches tall.

Culture

Corn must be planted in short blocks of four rows, rather than in a single long row, or even in two long rows. Since it is wind-pollinated, the plants need to be in reach of each other.

Late spring: Seeds should be planted around the date of the last spring frost, in short furrows 2 inches deep, four or six seeds to a foot. Each planted block should be at least 6 feet long, with four rows 2 feet apart. The corn should be covered with an inch of soil, and subsequently thinned to stand 10 to 14 inches apart. Corn can also be planted in clumps or hills, five seeds to each hill, 8 inches apart—the hills themselves should be 6 feet apart. When corn is to be grown this way, it is possible to cover the entire growing area after the hills are prepared with black plastic and plant the seed through slits. Black plastic will warm up the soil, keep it weed free, and also allow for earlier planting. Thinning of corn is extremely important to produce a good harvest; the suckers thrown up by the remaining plants need not be cut out. Corn needs plenty of organic matter incorporated where the seed is planted, as well as 5-10-10 fertilizer, which should be spread in a band on each side of each row at the rate of half a pound for 25 feet of row at the time of planting. The fertilizer spread should be a little deeper than the seed has been sown and at least 2 inches away from it. In poor to average soil this fertilizing should be repeated when the corn is 10 inches tall. I have a gardening friend who plants corn as a triple-rowed hedge all around the periphery of the plot with great success. Corn is shallow-

rooted and a thirsty plant. It grows best, therefore, surrounded by a heavy mulch. Since corn has to be planted fairly close in order to be safely pollinated, and since it grows into large plants, it is hard to do the midseason fertilizing if there is mulch or a black plastic layer down. Under those circumstances use a water-soluble fertilizer exactly according to directions when the corn is about 12 inches high.

Harvesting

When you pull back a bit of the husk and find the kernels are full, corn is ready for harvesting.

Ailments

Crows are a great nuisance, picking the corn seed out of the ground after it's planted and pulling young shoots out of the ground after they first germinate. There is not much that can be done about crows except to try a scarecrow or a mobile made from old tin cans that clash together, threaded on nylon fishing line. The noise of this, if it doesn't drive you crazy, will sometimes distract the crows. You can also suspend tin can lids or nails from a line running over the row of young seedlings.

The corn earworm or borer can be a nuisance and hard to handle. Red pepper dusted on the tassels is said to work well, but it never did very much for me. Sevin is most usually recommended as the right dust for the tassels as soon as they appear, and since bees do not visit corn, this is probably the one instance in which Sevin can be used without damage to bees. Rotenone dusted deep into the leaf axils and also on the corn tassels is a perfectly safe though not totally successful preventative against the ear borer. Even more troublesome in many areas are raccoons, which are almost impossible to keep out of a corn plot once they smell the ripening ears. I have found it impossible to grow enough corn to satisfy raccoons and have any left for myself. Raccoons can be controlled to a limited degree by trapping them alive in cage traps; at least that is the experience of a neighbor who deals with them in this way. The fact that he traps raccoons and removes them a considerable distance has, however, not saved *my* corn in the next field from further attacks! It is my experience, therefore, that once territory is vacated through man's interference by

trapping one raccoon family another set of raccoons will immediately move in, and start on your corn. Ruth Stout, that most excellent of gardeners, has found that an enclosed wire cage with a wire roof over the top, the type that the British use to protect their currants, is the only certain way to keep raccoons away from ripening corn. This would be a considerable, one-time expense, but might be very well worthwhile if a garden is incomplete for you without corn. But in that case the corn would always have to grow in exactly the same position, and it would be absolutely essential that at least 8 inches of fresh compost be rototilled into the soil every single season, along with a fresh supply of 5-10-10 fertilizer, either chemical or organic. I read that a transistor radio playing loudly in a corn crop all night will sometimes deter raccoons. This may be possible if you garden in deep country, but it would be very hard to bear in a suburban plot. I tried it once; it did not keep the raccoons off the corn, but it did bring me a still note from my neighbors.

Varieties

There are so very many varieties offered in the catalogs that it is extremely hard to give any advice. I found the dwarf types of corn hardly worth growing: the ears were too small to be of much use. *Golden Bantam* and *Golden Ridges* are still very popular varieties. Other gardeners suggest *Spring Gold, Golden and White Mixed.* For a single sowing that will bring you a succession of corn throughout the growing season, one excellent gardener recommends sowing simultaneously *Early Sunglow Hybrid, Butter and Sugar Extra Sweet,* and *Illini Xtra-Sweet* or *Iochief.* Many catalogs also offer a collection of early, midseason, and late corn that should all be sown at the same time.

CUCUMBERS

These are easy vines to grow as a home crop, and there will be a large return from only a few plants. There are varieties that do well in small containers, and many of these are listed in various catalogs. Hybrid seed that is resistant to some of the many diseases that attack cucumbers is by far the best buy,

though it will be a little more costly. Modern packaging of seed often consists of all female plants, known as gynoecious, which produces a much heavier yield. Very often in these all-female packaged seeds a few male plants, in which the seed is stained a different color, are included. If you are raising this seed at home, make sure that some male plants are sown at the same time and mark these with a label. When the seedlings are thinned out, always retain a few male plants in order to induce pollination. Some of the newest all-female packaged seed contains no male seed at all. These will bear fruit, but take care not to plant this variety anywhere near other cucumbers, or they will be cross-pollinated by the male flowers of the other plant, to the detriment of the taste of the all-female variety.

Culture

Cucumbers throw very deep roots and need plenty of fresh organic matter around their roots to do well. In large plots they can be grown in hills or groups and allowed to trail along the ground. In smaller plots they do best trained up a trellis (pages 64–65). For hill cucumbers dig out a hole 2 feet wide and at least a foot deep and set the soil aside. If you possess compost refill the hole at least three-quarters of the way up with fresh compost, and mix in a cupful of 10-10-10 fertilizer or 2 tablespoons of timed slow-release capsules. If you possess no compost, mix the soil that came out of the hole with damp peat moss or other organic matter, and add 2 cups of 10-10-10 or 3 tablespoons of timed-release capsules. Backfill the hole so that a mound stands a little above the soil surface. If cucumbers are to be grown on a trellis, dig a trench a foot deep, fill the bottom half with compost or other organic matter, and add 2 pounds of 5-10-10 or half a cup of timed-release fertilizer for every 25 feet of row. Backfill with the remaining soil so that the earth of the trench is mounded up. Allow the mound to settle for at least a week before either sowing or setting out cucumbers.

Three weeks before the last frost: Three weeks before the date of the last frost sow seed indoors in individual pots, three to a pot. Cucumbers are fussy about root disturbance, and do not like to be sown in flats. Thin to a single specimen in each

pot. The seeds should be sown on edge, half an inch below the soil surface. If using gynoecious seed, make sure male seed, if it appears in the package, is sown and carefully marked. Home cucumbers should be timed always to be able to be set out before they start to vine. If they've once started to elongate they will receive a severe setback when they are moved.

Two weeks after last frost: Two weeks after the average date of the last frost, around the time the pole beans and tomatoes are set out, sow cucumber seed outdoors, on its side, half an inch deep. Side seeding of this type prevents rot in the cold, damp soil, but seed will not germinate well if the air temperature is consistently under 55 degrees. In mounds, which should be 4 feet apart, sow six to eight seeds. Seeds for trellis growing should be sown 4 to 6 inches apart. Mound seeds should be thinned to three specimens; the trellis seeds should be thinned to stand 8 inches apart in the row. To deter the cucumber beetle sow some climbing nasturtium seed at the same time and at the same depth as the cucumber seed (see page 158). Thin these to one per mound and one for every foot of row along the trellis. I'm told that radish seed sown among cucumbers will ward off many pests, but of this I have no personal experience. Since radish is cheap and comes very quickly from seed, experimenting with this idea throughout the summer is well worth trying. Cucumber seed can be sown directly into outdoor containers that are filled with a very rich organic mix, or they can be moved into them after being raised indoors and properly hardened. Young cucumber seedlings are particularly resentful of drenching, cold spring rain: cover newly set-out or newly germinated plants with waxed milk cartons with most of the top still intact for protection if a spell of bad weather of this type sets in in early June. Cucumbers growing in a trench beside a trellis can also be covered with plastic sheeting thrown over the trellis and held down with stones. Cucumbers in containers should also be protected (pages 130–31). As the plants start to expand be very careful not to tread on or break off the growing tips of the vines, for this opens up an entry route for disease.

Early summer: Cucumbers should always be heavily mulched; this will conserve moisture and keep the fruit clean for those that are grown on the ground. If black plastic mulch is used, which will warm the soil up earlier, it must be in place before the cucumbers are set out in holes cut through it, and it will be necessary to water, fairly heavily, with a slow trickle through other holes cut in the plastic, in order to make sure the cucumbers get enough water. If cucumbers run short of moisture during their growing season, they cease to produce, but they will resume full production when they are thoroughly watered again. Because cucumbers are shallow-rooted, use care if cultivation is necessary.

Harvesting

The fruit can be harvested and eaten at almost any size, but cucumbers must not be allowed to remain on the vine to become absolutely enormous or to ripen. When this occurs, cropping will cease forever. Cucumbers will scramble up into hedges of their own accord, but this makes them hard to harvest, and it also shades the plants so that crop production is less profuse.

Ailments

Cucumbers are heirs to a tremendous number of diseases. Protected hybrid seed is, therefore, by far the best choice. Constant watch should be kept for aphids, which should be hosed off or treated with rotenone or pyrethrum. If malathion or Ortho-tomato and vegetable dust is used for either aphids or for the striped cucumber beetle, which is a big nuisance for these plants, the fruit must wait seven days before harvesting, and should not be eaten unpeeled no matter how thoroughly it is washed. The striped cucumber beetle carries cucumber wilt in its digestive system, and it is extremely important, if possible, to prevent this pest from ever getting a toehold among cucumber vines.

Varieties

Gynoecious: *Victory, Gemini.* Normal: *Burpee's Hybrid, China Long.* For containers: *Patio Piks* and many cucumbers mentioned in the Thompson and Morgan catalog. Pickling: *Pioneer, Wisconsin SMR 18, Burpee Pickler.*

Dill

DILL

This annual herb once grown in the plot has a tendency to reappear of its own accord. Dill, however, grows very large, from 2 to 3 feet high and equally wide. Self-sown dill may well not come up in an appropriate place. Since it is tap-rooted, dill cannot be transplanted, so regular seeding is advisable even where self-sown dill appears in a plot.

Culture

Very early spring: Dill does not mind acid soil, but it does need full sun and a soil very rich in organic matter. It can be sown in short rows, not more than ¼ inch deep, for any seed that self-sows naturally should never be deeply buried. Seed should be sown about 2 inches apart, thinned to stand 6 inches apart and then a foot apart if the plants are growing well. After tomatoes are set out, a row of dill should be planted in front of them to attract the tomatoworm. But if this strategy suc-

ceeds you will not get much use out of that particular row for culinary purposes! Otherwise resow dill every three weeks for a regular supply all summer. Dill, being so tall, is liable to be blown over in unprotected yards. Staking with thin bamboo stakes is advisable immediately after the second thinning. Planting in clumps helps keep dill from blowing over.

Harvesting

Leaves can be harvested at any stage, though it is sometimes said they are at their most aromatic as the flowers are just unfolding. The seed will not ripen until nearly two months after sowing, and should be picked and put into a bag before it is dispersed by the wind all over your garden.

Ailments

Nothing very much has ever bothered my dill, but I have had it grow rather poorly, in which case I usually run a side furrow along the row and pour in a light dressing of 5-10-10 and water this in thoroughly.

Varieties

There are two varieties of dill: *Bouquet* and *Long Island Mammouth.*

EGGPLANT

Eggplants need the same soil preparation as tomatoes, for they, too, are heavy feeders. They are short-season plants, but take a long time to germinate from seed and must be grown in warm soil with high air temperatures. They are unable to take the slightest touch of frost. Gardeners in growing areas with short seasons would do well to choose quick-maturing, smaller plants specially bred for northern gardens, and to raise these in containers in the sunniest, most sheltered position available. Again, as with tomatoes, the days to maturity noted on the package are counted from the time the plant is set outdoors. Novice gardeners would do well to buy prestarted eggplants, and even experienced gardeners often fall back on this method just so long as they are able to find the variety that suits their particular area. The time and trouble needed to raise eggplant indoors is not condu ive to easy home growing.

Culture

Eight to ten weeks before the last frost: Seeds should be started indoors, three seeds to an individual peat pot, one-quarter inch below the soil surface, in a soilless medium. After germination the seedlings should be thinned by clipping to the one strongest specimen. Eggplant needs high heat, 75 degrees by day and night to germinate, and germination itself will often take as much as three weeks. Once the plants are up, the air temperature should be slowly reduced, but this is not a plant that needs a very cool growing position, even indoors. Hardening off should be done extremely cautiously; the air in the cold frame, if that is where the plants are to be hardened, should never be allowed to fall below 50 degrees.

Early summer: When the day temperature is above or around 70 degrees set out the plants and do not plan to grow them anywhere near where tomatoes or peppers grew in a previous summer, or where they are to be grown this year. Eggplant is antipathetic to both these plants and suffers severely from a disease, verticillium wilt, which may be carried by tomatoes and peppers though it will not damage them nearly as severely as it damages eggplant. Ideally eggplant should always be grown in a different position each season. The reason for waiting so long before setting out the plants is their susceptibility to cold and the fact that if they find themselves even temporarily in an air temperature around the fifties, they will probably receive a setback from which they will not recover all season. Plants should be set 18 inches apart, and stakes should be in place before the plants are set out, for eggplants are particularly susceptible to any form of root disturbance. Eggplants need a great deal of moisture while they are growing and should be heavily mulched. After the fruit starts to set, pull the mulch away and spread a handful of 5-10-10 fertilizer in a ring around each plant, 10 inches away from the main stalk. Do not cultivate this in, for eggplant roots rather shallowly; water it in instead and then pull back the mulch. Keep the plants loosely tied to the stake as they develop. Eggplant is not only very easily knocked over by wind, but the weight of the ripening fruit drags it to the ground. If

the eggplant appears to be setting more than six fruit it is as well to pinch out the top to divert the plant's energy to fruit ripening.

Harvesting

Harvest the plants when they are about 5 inches in length and the skin still has a high gloss. Once the skin changes color and becomes dull the eggplant will taste bitter. Eggplant stems are woody and have to be cut off the plant; never attempt to pull them off, or serious damage will follow. Eggplants are excellent plants for containers, and they do very well in a sterile soil mix. With this mixture around their roots they will need feeding (pages 129–30), but there will be no danger of verticillium wilt.

Ailments

Flea beetles, red spider mites, and aphids are all a nuisance with eggplants and need to be controlled. This should be done by regular dusting with rotenone or pyrethrum. If verticillium wilt hits the eggplant there is no cure. The signs are the leaves wilting by day and, at first, recovering at night, but soon turning yellow and falling off. The only cure is prevention—that is to say, marking on your planning chart where this trouble is in the soil, and avoiding setting eggplant, tomatoes, and peppers in that particular area for the next three years, unless you buy verticillium-resistant seed.

Varieties

For northern areas, the short growing season: *Early Beauty, Jersey King, Early Wonder, Black Magic Hybrid, Nagaoka New Kissin* (Kitazawa Seed). In general: *Mission Bell, Royal Night.* In English and French catalogs look under "Aubergine."

GARLIC

Garlic, apart from its culinary use, also serves as a general pest repellent when it's planted freely throughout the vegetable plot. This method of growing garlic is practical in ground that is left under perpetual mulch and never cultivated, since the bulbs can be left deeply planted in position all winter to turn into larger and larger plants. In the second year garlic will throw up a white flower, and the bulb by then will have

matured sufficiently to be dug and used for culinary purposes in the late fall, and new small cloves replanted in its place. This is not, however, necessary, and the bulbs can be left in position to turn into enormous plants which can grow as tall as 3 feet. Most gardeners find this too large for their plots, and regular second-year replanting on a staggered schedule so that not all the big plants are removed the same year is the most practical way to use garlic as a pest repellent.

Culture

Very early spring: Plant individual cloves of garlic in rich, well-drained soil, with the tip of the clove about 2 inches below the soil surface. Garlic bulbs can be bought in garden centers and are usually much fresher than those bought for culinary purposes. Nevertheless, I've often used kitchen garlic cloves in my yard with success. If an early flower head is sent up, pinch this off in order to allow the bulb to develop.

Harvesting

The plant shows when it is ready to be dug when the green tops of the stems droop over on the ground.

Ailments

None.

Varieties

A giant garlic bulb called "Elephant" garlic exists which can be bought through seed catalogs and garden centers. This has much larger cloves and it is milder in taste than the species plant.

KALE

See "Collards and Kale."

KOHLRABI

This member of the cabbage family should be cautiously introduced to your own family, for though it has a pleasant, nutty taste, it is undoubtedly an acquired taste, and it's better to harvest a small one, around 2 inches in diameter, from a friend's plot for the initial venture! Kohlrabi sold commercially is usually so large so that it is woody and unappetizing. We are

not a kohlrabi family; I tried it once. After a single dish all the rest of the row had to be relegated to the compost pile—no one would touch it. As a result my experience is very limited, and my information largely comes from friends who have grown it.

Culture

Exactly the same as cabbage, except that kohlrabi has to be treated as a spring and subsequently as a fall crop. There is no strain that can carry on throughout the growing season.

Early spring and late August: Kohlrabi, which is very hardy, is best always started outdoors in the row where it is to mature. The seed should be sown half an inch deep and the seedlings thinned to stand 5 inches apart. Mulch should be pulled back as the bulb starts to swell.

Harvesting

Plants should be cut just below the swollen bulb level; pulling them will disturb the roots of the others nearby. Kohlrabi is ready about eight weeks after sowing, if it has been grown under mulch and kept regularly watered during dry periods.

Ailments

Same as for all the brassica-cole family (see "Broccoli").

Varieties

Early White Vienna, Early Purple Vienna.

LEEKS

This is a member of the onion family that does not bulb but forms a thick, cylinder-shaped stem. Leeks have a milder taste than onions and are excellent in soups and stews. The leek is, incidentally, the national emblem of Wales. The plants are slow growers that need rather special care and are not suited to a small plot. Those who love leeks, however, feel that a vegetable plot is not complete without them, particularly since this is a plant that will self-store happily in the ground in all but the most bitter climates.

Culture

Leeks, unlike other members of the onion family, are sensitive to overacid soil. Leeks grow best in a shallow trench,

around 6 inches deep, which should be dug out in the fall and the soil piled alongside the entire length of the trench. At that time 3 inches of organic matter, two handfuls of ground horticultural limestone, and two pounds of 5-10-10 for 25 feet of row should be well worked into the bottom of the open trench. In the spring the bottom of the trench must be thoroughly raked to make sure that it is clear of clods and stones to the depth of at least 4 inches. This is very important where good leek growing is involved.

Three months before the last spring frost: Many books suggest buying leek seedlings and setting these outdoors when the danger of frost is past. My friends who grow leeks sow leek seed indoors at a temperature of around 60 degrees, and they sow it very thickly. Germination is slow and uneven, and the seed should not be covered with more than a quarter inch of soil. The seedlings should be thinned by clipping very early to stand 2 inches apart, so as to provide uncrowded space for development.

Late spring: When the seedlings are about 4 inches tall they can be set out in the center of the trench. It is very important at this point to be careful not to break the single root which will be attached to the seedlings. The plants should be set 6 inches apart, and deep enough so that the point where the leaves branch in the stem is exactly at the level of the soil surface. The little plants can be held steady by patting a half-inch of soil against them on all sides. During the summer, continue piling soil up against the stalks of the leeks as the leaves expand. Be careful how this is done, but by working in this manner with the soil, weed growth will be kept down. When the entire trench is filled in, the area should be heavily mulched. Like all members of the onion family, leeks need plenty of moisture combined with good drainage. Piling earth against the stalks not only blanches them but also makes them tastier. I am assured that leeks grown without this slightly tedious pulling up of soil are always tougher and less tasty. Keep the trench heavily mulched, and if the soil is not naturally rich, fertilize in mid-July and again in mid-August with 2 pounds of 5-10-5 scattered in a 6-inch band along each side

of the plants for every 25 feet of row. Water, rather than
cultivate, this in.

Harvesting

Leeks are edible at any stage, but take about six full months
to reach full-size growth from seed. After the really cold
weather sets in, leeks should be covered with a heavy hay
mulch. They will then go safely through even the bitterest
winter and can be dug as needed.

Ailments

Same as onions.

Varieties

Odin, Giant Musselburgh, Conqueror (which is very cold resistant).

LETTUCE

For home vegetable gardening two types of lettuce are the
most rewarding: the butterhead type with a loose but quite
obvious head and the loose-leaf variety. All lettuce does best
in soil that is near the neutral mark. If you know your soil to
be very acid, spread a little ground limestone along the furrow
where lettuce seed is to be sown.

Culture

Lettuce is a cool-weather crop. It does best grown before
the weather heats up. Once the temperature goes regularly
over 70 degrees by day lettuce bolts, or runs to seed. It is best
to grow several early crops successively in short rows and then
start it up again in late August for fall harvesting. Lettuce needs
plenty of nitrogen for quick, succulent, leafy growth, and it
therefore needs a soil into which a lot of organic matter has
been incorporated. If lettuce seed is to be sown where a previous crop has already been harvested in that same season, 2
inches of compost or damp peat moss, together with a pound
of 10-10-10 and a couple of handfuls of ground horticultural
limestone, should be incorporated into the soil for every 25
feet of row. Lettuce needs plenty of moisture for good growth;
it does well under perpetual mulch, which keeps the leaves
from being soil spattered.

Six weeks to a month before the ground is workable:

Lettuce can be started indoors; the seed germinates easily at a temperature of around 60 degrees, with a very thin covering over the seed. Seedlings should be transplanted to stand 2 inches apart before they are over an inch high, and should be grown on in the coolest, brightest possible place indoors.

Very early spring: As soon as the soil is workable, hardened transplants should be set outdoors. Butterhead and Cos varieties should stand 8 inches apart, loose leaf 4 inches apart. At the same time, short rows of lettuce can be sown in the plot a quarter of an inch deep. These can be thinned twice, the first time by clipping out the unwanted seedlings, and the second by the mud method, which will provide transplants (pages 108–9).

Late August: For fall crops, lettuce seed can again be sown in late August, and at this stage the most shady position in the plot should be chosen. Lettuce will grow well even when crowded closely together, though the plants will be much smaller. Crowded plants, however, have a far greater tendency to bolt. Leaf lettuce is the most useful for hot climates as it is far less liable to run to seed, but leaf lettuce grown in very hot weather often becomes tough and coarse. Miniature varieties of lettuce can easily be grown in containers.

Ailments

None worth worrying about, but avoid evening wetting of foliage to avert rot and mildew. Slugs and snails can be a nuisance in the early stages (see page 154) as can occasional attacks of white fly (see page 156).

Varieties

Butterhead, Buttercrunch, Dark Green Boston, Dwarf Cos. Loose leaf: *Ruby, Black-seeded Simpson, Oak Leaf, Salad Bowl, Green Ice.* Miniature for containers: *Tom Thumb.*

MARJORAM

Marjoram is a tender perennial that is better treated as an annual.

Culture

Marjoram needs full sun, lime added to a soil that is naturally acid, and plenty of moisture. Novice gardeners can buy

young plants or seed can be sown outdoors about two weeks before the date of the last spring frost. Seed can be started indoors in the late winter.

Ailments

None that are likely to plague the average gardener.

MELONS

I have not had a great deal of luck with melons in the past in my vegetable plot. But my most recent method of growing this plant has been in 12-gallon containers in very warm sheltered positions, and this has been most successful. Growing melons in a protected sunny cold frame has also been very successful for many of my friends. According to Malcolm Cowley, writing in the January-February 1975 issue of *Country Journal,* the muskmelon, or cantaloupe, and small watermelons should be able to be grown, "anywhere where tomatoes can be harvested in quantity before mid-August." This is a reasonably accurate generalization with some very specific conditions. Melons are not, however, an easy crop; no matter what the books or catalogs may say, gardeners should not be discouraged if they fail. Most of us do, or have done so, sooner or later with melons.

Culture

Very early spring: Melons, to grow best, need rich, moisture-holding soil, heavily laced with compost, that drains well. They will not thrive in very acid soil. If they are to be grown in plots, holes should be dug a foot deep and 2 feet across, and the excavated soil piled on one side. The bottom of the hole should then be filled with compost or some form of organic matter into which a cupful of 5-10-10 has been mixed. If the organic matter is damp peat moss, a handful of ground horticultural limestone should also be mixed in with it. If the melons are to be set out in a row, the trench should be dug to the same depth and compost added in the same manner, as well as one pound of 5-10-10 for every 25 feet of row. Wood ashes are also excellent mixed into the bottom of the melon holes, but when wood ashes are used lime should be omitted. The soil

should be backfilled into the holes or trench, so that it is slightly mounded up, and the growing area then should be completely covered with black plastic mulch. Black plastic mulch serves the invaluable purpose of warming the soil; it also holds in moisture and keeps down weeds. Melons ripening on it do better because of the reflected heat, as well as from the warm soil in which their roots are reveling. The black plastic mulch must be very firmly anchored down with rocks or bricks. If earth is used to hold it down there will be a terrific growth of weeds on the earthen mounds, which may well harbor plant pests fatal to melons.

Four weeks before the last frost: Start melon seeds, three to a pot, in individual peat pots. Avoid Jiffy pellets, for they stay too wet. Set the seed on edge to be sure of avoiding rot. Melons need a temperature of around 70 degrees to germinate. Thin to the single strongest seedling in each pot, and be very careful with the hardening-off process. Melon seedlings should never be exposed to temperature under 50 degrees: it will give them a check from which they will not recover. The plants should not have started to vine before they are moved. About the time the tomatoes are set out, get a set of hot caps, those waxed paper tents you can buy at any garden center. Cut slits in the black plastic and set out the melons, being very careful not to disturb the roots. Water thoroughly through the slit in the plastic, and set the hot caps over the melons. Store-bought prestarted plants should be treated in an identical manner and should also be covered with hot caps. Where there is a long, hot growing season of more than three months of weather regularly over 75 degrees, melon seed can be started directly outdoors. Keep the hot caps in place until the night temperature remains above 55 degrees, but after they've been in position about ten days, cut off the tops to allow in more light and air. Seedling melons should not be more than two to a hill. The hills themselves should be 6 feet apart. With trench planting, cantaloupes should be 5 to 6 feet apart, watermelons 7 to 8 feet apart. With melons in containers any type of mulch material will do to cover the soil, but the container soil should be allowed to warm up very thoroughly before the mulch is

put down. Container seedlings should also be protected by hot caps or by half-gallon milk cartons until the night air is regularly above 55 degrees.

Midsummer: When the vines have spread over a foot in length, the plants should be fed with a water-soluble fertilizer, and this should be repeated a second time when the fruit begins to start. There should be no more feeding after the melons are the size of little marbles. I have had no luck growing melons on trellises, even though I have tried the trick of holding the fruit up in slings.

Harvesting

Melons are ripe when they slip freely off their stems when they are lifted up.

Ailments

Melons are extremely susceptible to fusarium wilt, and disease-resistant seed should be bought. Close watch should be kept for the striped cucumber beetle, which can be controlled with malathion or rotenone or an all-purpose vegetable dust. If the cucumber beetle gets on melons it will spread fusarium wilt through its digestive system.

Varieties

My only experience is with melons grown in the Northeast, and for this I and my friends have grown cantaloupes, *Burpee Hybrid, Harper Hybrid,* and a variety, *Delicious, 51,* which has some resistance to fusarium wilt.

MINT

There are innumerable varieties of mints, all of which spread with underground runners called stolons that are hard to control. Mint in a small plot is best planted in a slightly shady area (it does not enjoy full sun) in a spot formed by sinking a bottomless bucket or washtub deep into the soil. Novice gardeners would be wise to buy prestarted plants or ask a friend for a twitch of mint, which will always be available where anyone grows it.

Culture

Mint likes rich soil, full of organic matter, and plenty of

moisture during the growing season. If after three years the patch seems overcrowded the roots should be dug up and reset elsewhere, and all the small pieces of root that escape that digging should be ruthlessly eliminated.

Very early spring: Mint can be fed each spring with a dusting of balanced fertilizer, spread over the growing area, before any top growth shows.

Summer: Flowers should be pinched back to encourage plenty of leaf growth.

Ailments

Mints can have disease problems but these are unusual in home patches.

Varieties

For culinary purposes: *Spearmint (Mentha spicata),* the variety used with lamb and for making jelly or mint sauce. Also *Apple Mint (M. rotundifolia)* and *White Peppermint* (*M. piperita officinalis*).

ONIONS

This is a worthwhile long-season vegetable in a fair-size plot. In small plots, growing onions to maturity takes time and much-needed space for a vegetable that does not taste all that different from the commercial product. Fully mature, home-grown onions should also always be allowed to dry out for several days before being used since many people are highly allergic digestively to full-size, unripened onions. But every plot should grow small green onions which take up very little space and contribute enormously to the delicacy of home salads.

Culture

Onions need fertile, well-worked soil that is free of clods and stones, and they do not mind mildly acid soil conditions. The area where onions are to be grown should have an extra layer of compost or organic matter incorporated into it before planting, even if organic matter was also incorporated into the whole plot the previous fall. Onions are one of the few vegetables that can be grown for several years in the same position, and this makes very careful soil preparation well worthwhile.

Onions are particularly sensitive to poor drainage; in plots where this is a problem they should be grown on raised beds. Potash is extremely important to the development of onions, so wood ash is valuable incorporated into the soil where they are to grow.

February: Onions can be started indoors, but they will take two months to become large enough to transplant.

March: As soon as the ground can be worked, onion sets, which can be bought at garden stores or through catalogs, can also be set out. Onion sets are small onion bulbs that were grown from seed the previous year and kept small by very close, unthinned planting. Do not buy sets in which the bulbs are over half an inch in diameter, for these big bulbs are liable to run to seed rather than bulb. Sets can be planted in the furrow an inch deep and the top left uncovered. Around about the date of the last frost, sow onion seeds half an inch apart and a quarter-inch deep and barely cover the seed. Make sure, however, that the seed is in close contact with the soil. Start to thin as soon as the onion shoots appear. Ultimately the space between the plants should be about 6 inches. Onions rise out of the ground as they develop and sit on top of the soil. It is important to mulch up to the area where the plants are expected to bulb, but not right up to the stems themselves. It is also very important to keep weeds down in the row between the onions, as weed growth will interfere with the swelling of the onion bulbs. In average soil onions should be fertilized when the top growth is about 12 inches high. 5-10-10 should be used in a band after the mulch has been pulled away along each side of each row at the rate of half a pound for 25 feet of row. Onions are plants that are greatly affected by light hours. During the long days of early summer, all their energy goes into the green top-growth, and if flower shoots appear these should be cut out the very moment they are spotted. When the daylight hours begin to shorten, the bulb starts to expand, and this stage is marked by the cessation of any new top growth in the center of the plant.

May: Home-grown onion seedlings can be set out in rows in the garden 3 inches apart and then used as green thinnings

from July on. In addition to row planting, some of the seedlings should be set out in bunches, about six to a bunch. These will develop into scallions, which are also excellent for salad.

Harvesting

When the leaves start to yellow and fall down they should all be bent over by hand, pointing in the same direction. This will speed up the bulb-ripening process. When they are completely withered, the bulbs should be dug, air dried and stored in a well-ventilated area. In general, onion sets will be ready

Onions

three and a half months after they are set out. Onion seed will be ready five months after it was set out.

Ailments

Onion maggots can be a nuisance but are fairly unusual in home plots. Thrips in June and July are quite common. These suck the foliage and turn it yellow in color. They can be controlled with rotenone or malathion.

Varieties

Seed: *White Sweet Spanish, Southport White Globe.* Sets: *Zittau, Ebenezer, Yellow Bermuda,* and again *White Sweet Spanish.* Bunching (scallions): *Beltsville Bunching.* Storing: *Zittau, Sweet Spanish, Ebenezer.*

PARSLEY

Parsley always does best in a soil full of organic matter that has been raked free of clods and stones, and although it prefers full sun, it can take the moving shadow thrown by tall plants nearby. As an outdoor container plant parsley does well in a slightly shaded place; full sun on a patio may be too hot for it. Container-grown parsley needs a considerable amount of water.

Culture

Early spring: Seed can be sown a quarter-inch deep as soon as the ground is workable. Boiling water should be poured on the exposed seed as it lies in the furrow, which should then be covered with a quarter of an inch of soil. This treatment leads to faster, more even germination than soaking the seed in water overnight. The plants grow well even when crowded, but for big, individual plants, thin to 6 inches apart. Parsley is a biennial that often survives through mild winters. The second year, however, it throws up flower stalks and the leaves become bitter, so a new row of parsley should be sown each season. Parsley for the winter indoors can be handled by sowing seeds, treated with the boiling water, directly into pots in late August, or plants can be dug up after frost, the foliage cut back, and replanted in a very deep pot, for parsley throws a deep taproot. It can then be grown on in the coolest, sunniest

place you possess, and will give you plenty of parsley throughout the winter.

Ailments

There is a parsley root worm but it is unlikely to get into
the average home plot.

Varieties

Strongly flavored: *Dark Leaf Italian.* For garnishing: *Moss
Curled.*

PARSNIPS

This is a long-season vegetable that should remain in the
ground until there have been several fall frosts; otherwise the
roots, or parsnips, will not be sweet tasting. They can be left
late in the garden covered with a hay mulch and dug during
the course of the winter, or they can be left uncovered all
winter long, in which case they will survive perfectly happily
in this self-storage even in the coldest areas and then can be
dug and used in the spring.

Culture

Parsnips need a deep soil, raked free of clods and stones,
to a depth of at least 8 inches. This is the one essential difference between parsnips and other root vegetables—this necessity for deep, good tilth.

Early spring: The seed should be sown a couple of weeks
before the last air frost, in a furrow half an inch deep, and
should then receive the boiling water treatment (page 97). The
seeds then should be covered only very lightly, and preferably
with vermiculite, for they find it difficult to break through
hard, heat-crusted soil. Since the seed will be slow to germinate
even with the boiling treatment, it should always be sown
thickly. After germination the plants should be thinned to 4
inches apart. For good development it is important to keep the
rows weed-free. The area close to the row of seeded parsnips
should always be kept under heavy mulch.

Harvesting

As above, after the first fall frost, or in spring after a winter
of self-storage. Parsnips should always be dug, not pulled.

Ailments
None worth mentioning.
Varieties
Hollow Crown, All America, Harris Model.

PEAS

An excellent crop for a moderate-sized garden, though they take up rather too much room in small plots. But home-grown peas, like home-grown corn, taste so much better than anything that can be bought at the store that they are well worth trying, even for the novice gardener who has rather minimal room. The grower must be prepared to provide some kind of support (pages 64–65) to prevent the vines from spreading along the ground. Peas are particularly suitable for cool, late-season areas, for they will fail as soon as the weather has heated up and remains steadily over 70 degrees by day. Peas are classified as wrinkled or smooth, which is how the seed looks when dried. The wrinkled variety makes sweeter eating. Peas are often recommended for a midsummer sowing to bring a fall crop. I've had no success with this method.

Culture

Peas do best in a soil that has had 1 cup of ground limestone added for every 25 feet of row. A double row should always be planted 2 or 2½ feet apart. Peas can be easily supported with a wire trellis, but novice gardeners would be wise to avoid the very tall varieties. Snow or sugar peas—those that are eaten while they are still in the edible pod—are an excellent choice for smaller plots, because they really do need no staking. For gardeners who have plenty of room for peas, it is wise to plant early, midseason, and late varieties at the same time at a very early date in exactly the same way as the three seasons of corn are planted at the same time.

Very early spring: Peas should be sown just as soon as the ground can be worked, and if you have the time and energy, peas will grow best if a 3-inch trench is dug for them in the fall and plenty of organic matter incorporated into it. With acid soil, ground limestone should also be added in the fall. Fertil-

izer high in nitrogen should always be avoided with peas. Since peas add nitrogen to the soil, a nitrogen fertilizer will lead to vine growth at the expense of pods.

Early spring: If a trench has been dug, sow the seed down the center. If no trench was dug, make a furrow 2 inches deep and sow the seed about an inch apart. Peas do not mind reasonable crowding, and for a good crop plenty of vines are needed. The seed bed must have a flat base, so the seed should never be dropped into a V-shaped furrow. As soon as the plants are 3 inches above the ground, earth from the side of the trench or from the ground itself should be pulled up against them. This forms a simple early support, which is extremely important, for once pea vines are bent or injured, the crop they will bear is much more limited. Rows of peas also benefit from heavy mulching.

Harvesting

The lower pods on the rows will be ready first and should be harvested as the peas swell but before the seed itself becomes hard. Regular harvesting will prolong the crop in cool areas. Snow peas should be harvested as the pods begin to enlarge, but before the peas within them begin to swell. Once the pea hulls wither pull aside the mulch and remove all the debris. Spread 3 inches of compost and a pound of 5-10-10 along the row where they have grown and rake this in well. Peas are heavy feeders that will deplete the land for the successive crop. They do not, however, need extra fertilizer during their growing season.

Ailments

None worth mentioning, except aphids, which should be hosed off the moment they're seen.

Varieties

Early and dwarf: *Tiny Tim* and *Little Marvel.* Main crop: *Lincoln, Thomas Laxton, Recette, Tall Crop, Alaska.* Warm weather: *Wando.* Edible-podded: *Dwarf Gray Sugar, Burpee Sweetpod.*

PEPPERS (Sweet and Hot)

Peppers are excellent plants for growing in a small plot or

in containers, and with good handling will carry a profuse crop that can be harvested at any stage. Peppers should not be grown close to tomatoes or eggplants, or in the soil in which these plants grew in previous years.

Culture

Peppers need full sun and soil that is reasonably rich in organic matter. One inch of compost and one pound of 5-10-10 fertilizer should be worked into the soil in a 6-inch band for every 25 feet of row. Peppers can also be set in individual holes: dig out soil to a depth of 6 inches, add a 2-inch layer of compost and a cupful of 5-10-10, work this into the bottom layer, and then backfill around the plant. Too much nitrogen in the soil leads pepper plants to fail to set fruit. Peppers also cease to bear when the day temperature is over 90 degrees. If they are grown on hot patios, watch the thermometer and move the plants to a less sunny position during very hot spells. Peppers need moist soil around their roots and should have a thick organic mulch drawn up close to them. The plants should not be regularly flooded with water, since this brings on too much leaf growth, again at the expense of the crop.

Spring: Six to eight weeks before the days average 55 degrees temperature: start pepper seed indoors in individual containers, in a temperature of 75 degrees. Thin by clipping to one in each pot, and grow on in a warm, bright place. Harden off very carefully (see "Eggplant"). Novice gardeners would be well advised to buy prestarted plants.

Early Summer: After the temperature averages above 55 by day: set out the peppers in soil that has had the mulch drawn back from it in order to warm it up. The plants should be at least 18 inches apart, and stakes should be already in position before the plants are set out. Protect immediately from cutworms, and, if necessary, keep hot caps or milk cartons with the tops cut out over them for several days until the plants are acclimatized to outdoor life. As the weather warms up, pull the mulch back close to the peppers.

Harvesting

Peppers can be used long before they change color, and must always be cut, not pulled, from the stem.

Ailments

See "Eggplant." Peppers are also particularly vulnerable to both aphids and white fly. Rotenone or pyrethrum is the best control for these pests. With white fly the control should start the moment the pest is noticed. If malathion is used, wait seven days at the minimum before harvesting.

Varieties

Sweet: *California Wonder, Yolo Wonder, Canape.* Hot: *Large Cherry, Hungarian Wax, Long Red Cayenne.*

POTATOES

Potatoes are not really a crop for a small plot. They are not suitable for any area less than 2,000 square feet, since they take up a lot of space and are a long-season crop. For those with room, potatoes store well. A few potatoes are, however, always well worth growing in containers, in order to be able to harvest the tiny, new potatoes that are almost never commercially available.

Culture

Potatoes, a cool-season crop, need to be grown in full sunlight in plenty of room. They do best in a mellow, fertile soil that is well drained, and it is wise to shift their position from year after year. They do not like soil that has recently been limed, but they will respond to extra fertilizer: a pound and a half of 5-10-5 for every 25 feet of row in a rich soil and 2 or 2½ pounds in poor soil. It is, however, important that the fertilizer be thoroughly incorporated into the soil well ahead of planting, and that the seeds (which are small potatoes or sections that contain the sprouting eyes) never come into contact with the fertilizer itself.

Early spring: Seed potatoes with at least three eyes to a section should be planted about two weeks before the date of the last frost. If the weather is unusually wet or cold, planting should be delayed or the seed will rot. Potatoes are usually planted in furrows 6 inches wide and at least 4 inches deep, covered with 3 inches of soil. A deeper trench will produce a heavier crop. The seed should always be set 12 inches apart.

The eye should be placed upward. It is also possible to plant the seed on the ground in a deep trench and cover it with 3 inches of hay held down with a little soil, with half-decayed leaves, or with half-decayed compost. I read, though I have never done it, that it is also possible to lay the seed on spoiled hay that is just lying on top of the soil and cover it in just the same way. With hay planting the balanced fertilizer has to be stirred into the lower level of the hay, not into the area where the seed is to be set. Potatoes can also be grown under black plastic, but this I have not tried.

Summer: As the sprouts grow, either mound the earth up around them or pile more straw or leaves or half-decayed compost around them. The mounding material should be around 8 inches high. New potatoes form just below the soil or hay level on underground stems that rise above the seed potatoes. Roots form below the seed potato. It is important always to prevent light from reaching the forming potatoes, as this causes them to turn green and become inedible.

Harvesting

Tiny new potatoes can be harvested around the time the flowers are in bloom, usually two months from planting date. With soil-grown potatoes the earth can be dragged aside very carefully and the potatoes picked off, but this often results in serious damage to the plant. With hay-grown potatoes, the mulch can be very simply pulled aside and the small potatoes harvested; the mulch is then put back, and the plant will continue to produce. Potatoes will be fully mature after the foliage withers and begins to die down. They can then be dug, washed, and sun-dried undercover before being stored in a dark cellar in which the temperature is around 45 degrees.

Seed Potatoes

If you have grown your own potatoes, you can use a few that you have stored for next year's crop. Take something like a melon scoop (the little ball with which you scoop out sections of melon) and dig out a scoop of flesh that contains an eye. Dip the cut portion in sulphur to prevent rot and then set it out as usual. Never try to use store-bought potatoes as seed potatoes, for these will have been specially treated to prevent sprouting.

Sources for seed potatoes, certified stock, that should be always used the first time, for it has been inspected and is free from the various blights, are Geo. W. Park Seed Co., L. L. Olds Seed Co., Gurney Seed & Nursery Co., Earl May Seed & Nursery Co. (see pages 72–73).

Container Growing

Container-grown potatoes can be grown in 12-inch pots and in much larger tubs. In either case there should be very good drainage in the bottom of the container, over which should be put rich soil with good organic matter incorporated into it. A cupful of balanced fertilizer in the lower level of the soil is all that will be needed. Fill the container half full and then place a layer of hay or leaves or any kind of mulch over the soil. On top put the seed potato, and cover it with 3 inches of soil. As the sprouts begin to elongate, pile more soil or more hay on top. Potatoes can be harvested either by turning the whole pot out when the plant is in bloom and plucking off the tubers, or by pulling the mulch aside in big containers, harvesting the tubers, and then putting the mulch back.

Ailments

There are many blights, and for that reason use only treated, certified seed. Aphids are controlled by rotenone, pyrethrum, or malathion. Colorado potato beetles can be hand-picked off container-grown plants and the foliage then sprayed with rotenone. Methoxychlor should be used if potatoes are being grown on a very large scale, but there then must be a wait of at least fourteen days before harvesting.

Varieties

Early (for summer use): *Early Gem, Irish Cobbler, Superior, Red Pontiac.* Late (for storage): *Russet, Burbank.* Potatoes are hard crops to recommend in general, and it is better to apply to your local county agricultural service to find the varieties best suited for your area.

RADISHES

The radish is a quick-growing crop that is sometimes used mixed in with slow-germinating seed to mark the row and thus

prevent an impatient or forgetful gardener from trying to plant something else in the same place. Radishes are good-natured and will usually produce some kind of root under any circumstances. They are, however, basically a cool-weather plant and should be grown early in the spring and again in the fall when the temperature curve is falling and not all through the season.

Culture

Radishes will grow almost anywhere and in any kind of soil. They are an excellent vegetable for children to start off with. To be more succulent, radishes should be sown in well-prepared soil that has been deeply dug and has plenty of organic matter in it. They also need to be kept plentifully supplied with moisture. Short rows can be started every ten days.

Very early spring: Radish seed can be started in many areas of the vegetable plot, since it takes less than a month to reach an edible size. One way to use it successfully is to plant a row where the hot-weather crops are to go later in the season. Seed should be sown ½ inch deep and thinned to stand an inch apart.

Harvesting

Radishes taste far better eaten young and small, rather than big and tough.

Ailments

Cabbageworm. Occasionally vulnerable to root maggots. Dust with rotenone or pyrethrum or *Bacillus thüringiensis.*

Varieties

Round and red: *Cherry Belle.* Long and white: *Icicle.*

RHUBARB

This is a perennial plant that should not be planted in the plot itself but treated as a decorative feature in a sunny spot elsewhere in the garden. For those who grow asparagus, a clump of rhubarb can be used as an exclamation mark at the end of each trench. The soil preparation for asparagus exactly suits rhubarb. To succeed, rhubarb must experience freezing weather each winter.

Culture

Most rhubarb is bought as plants from a garden center.

Roots will take a year before they are ready to harvest, seed at least two years.

Early spring: To prepare a place where rhubarb will grow for many years, dig a big hole 2 feet by 2 feet and fill in the bottom 6 to 8 inches with half-decayed compost or with some form of organic matter mixed half and half with the topsoil taken from the hole. Add to this one-third cup 10-10-10 fertilizer, or one-quarter cup of slow, timed-release fertilizer. Firm the soil down, add a little more on top, and then set out the plant (the bud upward) and cover with 3 inches of soil. A year-round mulch will conserve moisture, which rhubarb needs. When the new growth first appears, spread half a pound of 10-10-10 into the area around the little shoots and scratch it in thoroughly. This should be done every spring. Divide the roots about every third year in very early spring, just as the first shoots appear.

Fall: Each fall, after frost has killed the leaves, pull back the mulch and spread a 2-inch layer of compost over the plant. Replace the mulch lightly, and do not remulch heavily until after the spring fertilizer is on.

Harvesting

Stalks can be harvested from the second year on when they are 2 inches wide and around 4 inches tall. Leave narrow stalks alone to grow and send back strength to the root system. Always harvest by pulling and twisting simultaneously, and never pick all the leaf stalks on any plant. Rhubarb is a very decorative plant, but it should be prevented ever from going to seed by cutting out the flowering stalks during the summer, since this exhausts the root system. The leaves, as they unfold, are poisonous. The clumps are very long-lived.

Ailments

None that will commonly affect the home gardener.

Varieties

Red-stemmed: *MacDonald Red.* Green-stemmed: *Victoria.*

ROSEMARY

This is a tender perennial culinary herb that is best grown as a pot plant in a container on a sunny patio where the winters

are cold, since it is frost tender and will need to come indoors in winter. It is possible to sink rosemary in its pot in the soil outdoors, which will cut down on summer care. If it is planted outdoors, it must be lifted and repotted and brought indoors, or fresh cuttings should be taken in the fall.

Culture
Rosemary thrives in poor soil; it does not like overacid soil. It needs strong sunlight. It does not need a lot of water even when container grown.

Ailments
White fly and mealy bug can bother rosemary indoors but rarely attack it outside.

RUTABAGA
See "Turnip."

SAGE
Sage is a hardy perennial culinary herb.

Culture
Sage likes lean, well-drained soil and demands full sun. Overwatering can give this herb a great deal of trouble and may even cause mildew problems. Sage is more tolerant about acid soil than many herbs. Novice gardeners will do well to buy prestarted plants, but sage can be sown from seed indoors or outdoors in a short row, both in very early spring. The seedlings can be thinned or transplanted 12 inches apart, when they are 3 inches tall. From seed they will take two years to reach a harvestable stage. In the fall, sage foliage can be cut back when the garden is being put down for the winter.

Ailments
None likely to hit the home gardener.

SAVORY (SUMMER)
This is an annual plant easily grown from seed.

Culture
Savory is not very tolerant of overacid soil and should have

a sprinkling of lime in the seed furrow. The seed should be sown where it is to grow, in rich soil and in full sun. Seedlings should be thinned to stand 12 inches apart. Summer savory makes an excellent container plant if you are short of space.

Harvesting

Savory's small, narrow leaves grow in pairs along the stems. It does not produce enough leaves for an all-season harvest, so, like dill, there should be several successive sowings. Make cuttings before flowers appear if you plan to dry the leaves.

SHALLOTS

These are a very particularly delicate-tasting onion much favored by gourmet cooks. Like garlic, a single bulb will increase into a large clump of many small bulbs.

Culture

Shallots are usually grown from sets, and their culture is identical with that of onion sets. They should be planted 4 inches apart to allow the bulbs to multiply without pressure. Shallots are a perennial plant and can be left in the ground all winter. It's better to harvest shallots when the bulb has thickened up so much with the formation of new bulbils that the planting forms a noticeable mound above ground.

Ailments

Same as onions.

SPINACH

True Spinach

Spinach is a cool-weather crop, and sometimes it's worth taking a chance and sowing it in very late fall, just before the ground freezes. Quite often spinach seed treated this way will come safely through even the hardest winter, if there has been deep snow covering, and will appear very early in spring. Spinach is the best vegetable to use for intercropping in the front of areas where the hot-weather plants are later to be set out, since it will be finished and harvested long before later plants

start to spread. Spinach can also be grown as a fall crop, but this is by no means always a success, at any rate with me.

Culture

Spinach grows best in a nearly neutral soil. In areas where rhododendrons flourish a handful of ground agricultural limestone should be incorporated into every 25 feet of row if no soil test has been made.

Very early spring: As soon as the ground can be worked, spinach should be sown in furrows half an inch deep. When the seedlings appear, thin to stand 3 inches apart. When the leaves again touch, pull every other plant, which by that time should have reached an edible size. For gardeners in short-season, cool climates, spinach should be thinned to stand nearly 10 inches apart. The plants will then turn into very large specimens in which the leaves can be harvested rather than pulling the whole plant out. Wide spacing is also thought slightly to deter spinach from bolting to seed, when and if the weather warms up. The tendency of spinach to run to seed is as much affected by the lengthening of the daylight hours and the period of time it had to endure very cold air temperature after germination as it is by the heat of the daytime air. The so-called long-standing, or slow-bolting, varieties are always the best choice for spring growing everywhere because of these complicating factors. Spinach, being a leafy crop, needs an excellent supply of nitrogen. If a great deal of organic matter has not been incorporated into the soil, a nitrogen fertilizer should be sprinkled alongside the row on both sides when the plants are thinned for the second time, or one tablespoon of fish emulsion per gallon of water should be watered in around the roots of the plants. New plantings should be made every 10 days until the day temperature rises above 70 degrees regularly and sown again in late August for fall harvesting. Spinach needs plenty of moisture and should be grown with its roots well mulched. It is a plant that can also stand slight shade and can be safely put in the least sunny area of the plot.

Harvesting

Where spinach is being used as a quick crop in advance of later, tender plants, it should be pulled as soon as it reaches an

edible stage. Short-season gardeners may be able to grow individual plants long enough to make leaves suitable for harvesting rather than the whole plant.

Ailments

Aphids: control by rotenone and pyrethrum. Downy mildew and spinach yellows are both much more likely to appear in fall-grown varieties than in the spring crops. If these hit my plants, I pull them out.

Varieties

Spring: *Long-standing Bloomsdale, Winter Bloomsdale, America.* Fall: *Hybrid No. 7, Hybrid No 8,* which are blight and mildew resistant.

Malabar Spinach

This is a climbing plant that is not a true spinach but has succulent, dark green leaves that look like smooth spinach. It thrives extremely well in hot weather. It is quick growing and should be set against a fence or trellis up which it will scramble. It will not bolt, and in a recent test in Iran where the day temperatures went up to 115° for several weeks on end Malabar spinach throve and produced abundantly.

Harvesting

Use young leaves and tips for the new shoots.

Varieties

Burpee's Malabar.

New Zealand Spinach

Yet another false spinach, but a plant that resembles it in taste, and loves hot weather. Seed is very slow to germinate and should be soaked at least twenty-four hours before planting.

Four weeks before the last frost: New Zealand spinach can be sown indoors in a temperature of 60 degrees in individual containers. The plant is a relation of beet and chard, and several seeds will germinate from a single seed. Plants in containers should, therefore, be thinned by clipping to a single strong specimen.

A week before the last frost: Two weeks before the last spring frost, pull back the mulch to allow the soil to warm up.

Seed can then be sown in place in a furrow one inch deep and either thinned or transplanted by the mud method (pages 108–9) to stand 2 feet apart.   At this same period house-raised spinach can also be planted outdoors. New Zealand spinach develops into a tall, big, spreading plant.

Harvesting

The growing tips and the leaves nearest to the spreading tips can be harvested about two months from the date the plants went outdoors. The more these plants are cut back, the more profusely they will perform. Tips 3 to 4 inches long make the best clippings.

Ailments

None worth mentioning.

SQUASH

Squashes come in two kinds: the summer squash, including zucchini, which have to be harvested while they're immature and kept harvested in order that the bush will continue bearing, and winter squash, which is best harvested when mature after a touch of frost has browned the vines. With all squashes the bush type is the most useful for a small plot, for these do not take up nearly the amount of space of the old-fashioned vining types.

Culture

Squash needs full sun and a soil prepared in exactly the same way as for cucumbers. They should be grown under thick mulch and need steady moisture around their roots, but should not be flooded with water.

When day temperature rises above 55 degrees: Squash can be sown outdoors around the time the hot-weather plants are set out. It is possible to start it indoors earlier, but squashes are very sensitive to root disturbances at transplanting time. Six seeds can be planted to each hill an inch deep and then thinned to three strong specimens. If squash is planted in rows, the seed should be sown 1 inch deep and 6 inches apart. Plants should then be thinned to 18 inches or more apart.

Container Growing

Bush types of squash also grow excellently in containers.

Two plants in a 12-gallon container have done very well for me. Containers must have a layer of stones for good drainage, and the soil should be rich with organic matter. If there is space, winter squash that vine can also be successfully grown in containers. The vines will slowly spread over the edge of the container and then can be allowed to run about on the mulched ground nearby.

Harvesting

The crops must always be cut, not pulled. Summer squash or zucchini should be cut when it is very small—5 to 6 inches is the longest advisable size—and the skin should still be easily penetrated by the thumbnail. The crop should be regularly culled and cut to keep the plants producing. For storage, winter squash should not be picked until the vines are dead.

Ailments

See "Cucumbers." Also there is a squash borer that gets into the hollow stalks of squash. When a length suddenly wilts, look for a hole pierced in the stalk just below the point where the vine has wilted; slit the stalk open very carefully, and the grub will be there to be extracted and killed. After any such operation, dust the wounded end with rotenone so as to prevent the entry of the cucumber beetle.

Varieties

Summer, bush type: *Bush Cocozelle, Burpee Hybrid Zucchini* (which is also called *Zucchini Elite), Royal Acorn, St. Pat's Scallop, Patty Pan.* Winter, bush type: *Gold Nugget, Buttercup, Butternut, Hubbard, Table King,* and *Royal Acorn.* Royal Acorn is, in fact, a winter squash, but it can be used at an immature stage like summer squash.

TARRAGON

Tarragon is a perennial culinary herb.

Culture

Tarragon will grow in either sun or light shade, but does need considerable warmth. It can take a mildly acid soil, but prefers this not to be too rich. If the soil is very rich, the leaves will lack flavor. There is a problem about getting the right variety of tarragon. Seed is always the Russian tarragon, which

is not nearly such an aromatic plant. For that reason gardeners will always be wise to buy prestarted plants of the French tarragon *Artemesia dracunculus*. Especially good stock is available and can be shipped from the White Flower Farm, Litchfield, Conn. 06759. Tarragon will survive quite rough handling and left alone will grow so large that it needs staking. To prevent this, tarragon should either be divided every other spring or be severely root-pruned in the fall. In cold climates, it should be covered in winter.

Ailments
None worth mentioning in the average garden plot.

THYME

Thyme is a hardy perennial with many varieties. The common thyme is most often used for flavoring purposes.

Culture
Thyme needs a light, dry soil and plenty of sunshine. In areas where the soil is acid, ground limestone should be added. It withstands drought periods without a great deal of extra watering. Thyme grows particularly well in the pockets of cement blocks, for it enjoys the equivalent of rocks to scramble over. Thyme can also be grown in containers. It can be grown easily from seed, from cuttings, or by division from old plants.

Ailments
None likely to plague the average home gardener.

TOMATOES

Tomatoes are an excellent choice for both novice and experienced home gardeners. They can be satisfactorily grown in containers, in the vegetable plot, or in a sunny place elsewhere in the yard.

Culture
Deeply dug, well-prepared soil, good drainage, plenty of moisture on a regular basis, and full sunlight. Tomatoes can be grown with as little as six hours of full sun daily, but with that minimum sunlight the crop will not be large.

Fall: To grow tomatoes well, the ground should be prepared in the fall with deep digging that goes down 6 inches. A layer of 2 inches of compost or half-decayed organic matter should be added to the soil when the area is dug. If this is not available, 2 inches of damp peat moss should be used in its place. After digging, cover the area with a 6-inch layer of leaves held down with chicken wire.

Very early spring: Two months before the date in your area when the night temperature can be relied upon to remain above 55 degrees, check which growers in your area are raising prestarted tomato plants, and place an order. If you want to grow your own plants (pages 135 ff.) order seed that is marked as hybrid and has the letters "VF" or, preferably, "VFN" after it. This means that the plants from that seed are resistant to verticillium and fusarium wilt and root nematodes, all diseases fatal to tomatoes. Tomato seed should be started early (eight weeks before the date of the last frost) and moved regularly into bigger pots so that the plants are in a 6-inch pot when they are set out. This gives them a fine head start on much smaller, commercially grown plants.

As soon as it is possible to work outdoors, pull back the mulch and rake in 5-10-10 or 5-10-5 fertilizer (1 pound for every 25 feet of row) in a 6-inch-wide band. Water heavily and put back the mulch. If an organic fertilizer is used, you will need twice as much. If there was no fall soil preparation, dig holes 2 feet wide and 6 inches deep at a minimum of 3-foot intervals for each potential plant. Fill the bottom of the hole with compost into which has been mixed a tablespoon of superphosphate, a handful of 5-10-10, or a trowelful of bone meal. Add compost to the soil with which the hole is backfilled. If no compost is available, use damp peat moss. If the plants are to be staked or trellis-grown, set these supports up.

Two weeks before the average last frost date: Pull back the mulch to allow the soil to warm up. Do not set out plants until after the date when frost can be expected. Set out plants (pages 103–5), protect from cutworms (pages 107–8), and listen to the weather reports—also watch the thermometer. If the tem-

perature falls below 50 degrees, protect the plants (pages 63–64). After the plants are established and starting to develop, mulch heavily 4 to 6 inches deep over all the ground, as far as 6 inches away from the main stem. If the mulch is to be black plastic, this must be secured in place with bricks or stones *before* the plants are set out through slits cut in the plastic.

Types

"Early" tomatoes are determinate plants, which will grow to a fixed-size crop and die. These can be pinched to a single stalk and tied to a stake for the earliest possible ripening date. They can also be allowed to sprawl unpruned on the ground, since they will not take up much space, or be supported by low chicken wire cages. "Early" varieties should be planted 18 inches apart.

"Main-crop" tomatoes are indeterminate plants that will grow unceasingly unless deliberately stopped by the grower. Do so by cutting off the growing tips when they reach about 5 feet in height. Main-crop plants grown in a small yard do best if pruned to 3 stems and tied to a trellis. The pruning consists of allowing the two lowest shoots that appear in the leaf axils to remain and turn into fruiting stems that are also tied in. The shoots grow in the crotch where a leaf stalk meets the main stem. Except for those that are to remain, all the others should be snapped out with a downward motion while they are still small. Suckers that appear at the base of the plant should be cut out. Main-crop tomatoes can also be grown unpruned in wire cages (page 66). The cages should be set around the plants after the ground has been heavily mulched and after there is no further likelihood of frost. Further growth of caged tomatoes should be stopped by cutting off the growing points when the stems hang halfway down the outside of the cage. Unpruned main-crop tomatoes allowed to sprawl on the ground will each take up about 9 square feet.

Fertilizing

With proper advance soil preparation and heavy mulching, no extra fertilizer should be needed during the growing season. If the rainfall is normal and weather otherwise fine and there is still no fruit set 6-8 weeks after the plants have been set

Tomato Pruning

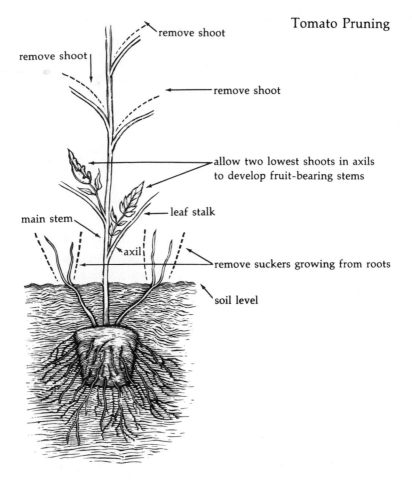

remove shoot

remove shoot

remove shoot

allow two lowest shoots in axils to develop fruit-bearing stems

main stem

leaf stalk

axil

remove suckers growing from roots

soil level

out, spread a band of 5-10-10 or 5-10-5 like light snow around each plant and rake that in under the mulch. Too much water and too much extra fertilizer, however, can prevent fruit set.

Ailments

Tomatoes are heir to all manner of ills in addition to those to which resistance has been bred. For those who spray, Captan or Maneb for disease control, Zineb and malathion for white fly and aphids, will take care of most problems. Never eat the fruit until two weeks after spraying, and even then wash the

skins very thoroughly. Never use systemic pesticides with any vegetable.

For those who do not spray, hard hosing with cold water under the foliage will take care of aphids and most of a bad attack of white fly. Do this job early on a hot day, so that the foliage does not remain wet during a humid hot night, since this is the route to mildew. Huge green tomato caterpillars must be hand-picked. Despite brilliant camouflage they can usually be found near an area where the leaves are all tattered. If not killed, they will destroy the crop.

I have found that growing protected hybrid seed in rich well-prepared soil in a fresh place each year, where the plants get full sun, has warded off almost all problems. In spite of the tomato's potential for disease, most home gardeners will harvest a fine crop without the use of violent poisons.

Harvesting

Pick unripe tomatoes in advance of early frost. These ripen quickly on a sunny windowsill, more slowly if they are stored in a cool, dark place and either placed on a shelf so they don't touch each other or wrapped individually in newspaper. Hanging the entire plant, roots and all, upside down is recommended by some as a means of post-season fruit ripening, but the fruit is very likely to fall off and be damaged before it can be picked. Excess tomatoes are easily canned, for, unlike most vegetables, they contain sufficient acid to be safely processed in a water bath. Normally freezing is not recommended for tomatoes, but I have had success in freezing them whole and raw for use in salads.

Varieties

Different varieties grow well in different areas. Gardeners should inquire of local growers and local garden centers. County agricultural services and state extension services will also supply this information. My friends and I have had success in the Northeast with *Small Fry, Pixie,* and *Patio* for containers; *Springset, Burpee VF Hybrid,* and *Moreton Hybrid* for "earlies"; *Better Boy* and *Big Boy* as main-croppers. There also exist many other types of tomatoes, including less acid yellow varieties and small cherry and plum types.

TURNIPS AND RUTABAGAS

These are root vegetables that can be grown for their green tops, particularly in the case of rutabaga, in cool weather, so in the small plot they must serve as either spring or fall crops. It has been my experience that both are easier to handle in the fall when the temperature curve is falling than in the spring. Turnips are smaller than rutabagas and mature faster.

Culture

Turnips and rutabagas are crops that dislike an acid soil. If your garden is in an area where rhododendrons flourish, and the soil has not been tested, scatter two handfuls of ground horticultural limestone for every 25 feet of row, and rake this in very thoroughly. The soil should be free of clods and stones for a depth of 6 inches.

Very early spring: Turnips and rutabagas should be sown, as soon as the ground can be worked, one-half inch deep and covered very slightly. One of the problems with seed germination of this plant is burying it too deeply. As soon as the seedlings germinate, they should be thinned to stand an inch apart. Turnips should be thinned a second time to stand 4 inches apart, rutabagas 5 inches.

Midsummer: Both plants can be resown for fall crops.

Harvesting

Turnips will be far tastier if they are harvested when they are around 2 inches in diameter. Rutabagas can be allowed to grow a little larger. Turnips are not frost-hardy and must be eaten before the cold weather freezes the ground hard; they also store poorly. Rutabaga is more hardy and can be left in the ground after the first frosts hit. It also stores far better.

Ailments

All the same as afflict other members of the brassica-cabbage family (see "Broccoli").

Varieties

Turnips: *White Globe.* Rutabagas: *Yellow Globe*

Index

Note: Page references in boldface indicate major treatment of the subject.

iv

A Note About the Author

Thalassa Cruso was born in 1909 and spent most of her childhood in Guildford, Surrey. She was trained in archaeology and anthropology at the London School of Economics, where she took an honors diploma in 1931. After apprenticing under Sir Mortimer Wheeler at Verulamium (St. Albans) and Professor Christopher Hawkes at Colchester, she excavated and published a report on the Iron Age Fort at Bredon Hill in Worcestershire. From 1931 to 1935 she was an Assistant Keeper at the London Museum in charge of the Costume and Nineteenth-Century Collections and the author of a book on costume. During World War II she served at the British Consulate in Boston where she has lived since her marriage in 1935. Throughout her varied career she has maintained an active interest in horticulture. In the fall of 1967 she launched a very successful television career with the 54-show series "Making Things Grow" on WGBH-TV (Boston), which is still running on public television across the United States. Since then her public television work has included the 36-show series "Making Things Work," a 6-part show on the "Small City Garden," WGBH Specials on the Flower Show in 1969, the Arnold Arboretum in 1972, and the Cape Cod Dunes in 1974, and, in 1974-75, commentary for "Family at War," a 53-part series sponsored by the Eastern Educational Network. In addition to her books she is a regular columnist for the *Boston Sunday Globe,* the *Boston Globe Calendar* and *McCalls Magazine* and a contributor to *Country Journal.* She is a Fellow of the Society of Antiquaries of London, a member of the Royal Archaeological Institute, the Royal Horticultural Society, the Garden Club of America, the Garden Federation of Massachusetts, and a trustee of the Massachusetts Horticultural Society. An accredited horticultural judge, she is herself the winner of many gardening and greenhouse awards, including, in 1969, the Garden Club of America's Medal of Merit, and, in 1970, the Horticultural Society of New York's citation for distinguished horticultural service and the Garden Club of America's Distinguished Service Medal.

A Note About the Type

The text of this book was set in Compano, the film version of Palatino, a type face designed by the noted German typographer Herman Zapf. Named after Giovambattista Palatino, a writing master of Renaissance Italy, Palatino was the first of Zapf's type faces to be introduced to America. The first designs for the face were made in 1948, and the fonts for the complete face were issued between 1950 and 1952. Like all Zapf-designed type faces, Palatino is beautifully balanced and exceedingly readable.